THE GREAT ATLANTIC CANADA BUCKET LIST

ONE-OF-A-KIND TRAVEL EXPERIENCES

ROBIN ESROCK

DUNDURN
TORONTO

For Abigail and Erin Kalmek

Library and Archives Canada Cataloguing in Publication
Esrock, Robin, 1974-, author

The great Atlantic Canada bucket list : one-of-a-kind travel experiences / Robin Esrock.

Issued in print and electronic formats.
ISBN 978-1-4597-2971-1 (pbk.).--ISBN 978-1-4597-2972-8 (pdf).--
ISBN 978-1-4597-2973-5 (epub)

1. Atlantic Provinces--Guidebooks. 2. Esrock, Robin, 1974- --Travel--Atlantic Provinces.
3. Atlantic Provinces--Description and travel. I. Title.

FC2004.E86 2015 917.1504'5 C2014-907089-6
C2014-907090-X

Editor: Allison Hirst
Cover and text concept: Tania Craan
Cover design: Courtney Horner
Text design: Laura Boyle
Cover images: Jon Rothbart; Peter C.; Ed English; Robin Esrock; Robin Esrock; Thinkstock; Robin Esrock; Linkum Tours (back cover)

1 2 3 4 5 19 18 17 16 15

We acknowledge the support of the **Canada Council for the Arts** and the **Ontario Arts Council** for our publishing program. We also acknowledge the financial support of the **Government of Canada** through the **Canada Book Fund** and **Livres Canada Books**, and the **Government of Ontario** through the **Ontario Book Publishing Tax Credit** and the **Ontario Media Development Corporation**.

Printed and bound in Canada.

Visit us at
Dundurn.com | @dundurnpress | Facebook.com/dundurnpress | Pinterest.com/dundurnpress

Dundurn
3 Church Street, Suite 500
Toronto, Ontario, Canada
M5E 1M2

CONTENTS

INTRODUCTION

It's my fourth year researching Atlantic Canada, and the deeper I dig, the more experiences I find. This afternoon, for example, I was in an underground coalmine, part of a museum honouring the history of mining in Cape Breton. Our guide, a coal-mining veteran, described an era when ponies pulled carts and blackened workers toiled six days a week in precarious conditions. A fascinating experience, and well worth the visit, but does it belong in *The Great Atlantic Canada Bucket List*? Is this truly something to do in Canada before you die?

I have visited over one hundred countries in pursuit of my bucket list. Along the way, I've realized that bucket lists are much like a game of whack-a-mole. You tick one experience off at the top, and three more pop up at the bottom. But in this book, I am effectively stating: *You must do this before you die*. It's a bold statement, fitting for subjects as wondrous and frightening as dreams and mortality. One morning, biking to work, a car jumped a stop sign and crashed into me. I hobbled away with a broken kneecap, a painful reminder of the gift of life, and the necessary motivation to finally tick off my own bucket list.

My adventures led to an unexpected career in travel journalism and television, allowing me to see more, and do more, than I could have ever imagined. Inspired by one of my columns in *The Globe and Mail,* I realized, however, that my travels had largely neglected my adopted home — Canada. And so began another journey, this time to every province and territory in search of the experiences one must do, and can only do, in Canada, before you die. Bucket lists, of course, are as different as the people who create them, but my selection criteria were simple: Is it unique to Canada? Can anyone and everyone do it? Is this something you'd remember for the rest

of your life? Tick all three boxes, and it made my shortlist. There's no meeting rock stars, no winning the lottery, and no unlikely fantasies, however dreamy they may be. Rather, I've created a practical Canadian bucket list — spanning adventure, history, culture, and food — all found in abundance in Canada's Atlantic provinces.

Atlantic Canada has no shortage of one-of-a-kind experiences. It is a region of immense beauty, with a culture as lively as a foot-stomping fiddle jig. Activities and destinations that might seem ho-hum to locals amaze us *come-from-aways*, whether we're driving on some of the world's most beautiful roads, catching and tasting local seafood, hiking in the forests, or visiting a museum. Take it from me, there are few places where you can walk headfirst off a cliff, kayak around an iceberg, or raft an actual tidal wave. In underrated New Brunswick, I walked the seabed beneath the Hopewell Rocks, and ziplined across one of Canada's largest waterfalls. Cycling across Prince Edward Island's Confederation Trail, the island's gentle beauty often applied the brakes. I drove across Labrador, picked bakeapples on rugged islands, and plucked my own "bergy bits" in Newfoundland. Nova Scotia's history is as fascinating as its coastal beauty, from the highlands of Cape Breton to the UNESCO World Heritage Site of Lunenburg.

Although you might have found this book in the travel section of your local bookstore, you'll quickly realize it's not a traditional guidebook. Rather than focusing on prices and meal recommendations — many of which will change before this book even goes to print

— I've focused on *why* you should visit these destinations in the first place. You're holding a personal journey into the very best of Atlantic Canada, and the joys and wonders that await us all. Accompanying this book is a comprehensive website with all the information you'll need to get started. At the bottom of each chapter, follow the website link to find practical information, links, meal and accommodation recommendations, videos, galleries, maps, and suggested reading guides. You'll also find regular blog updates, tips and commentary, and a chance to share your own experiences. Up-to-date information might be great online, but inspiration has always worked wonders on the printed (or digital) page.

One might argue that every national park, historic site, major city, or museum belongs on Canada's bucket list, and they would be right. In these pages you will find some obvious choices, some head-scratching facts, and a few laughs, too. It's an honour to be your guide, and it's a role I take seriously (although not too seriously, because if there's one thing Atlantic Canada has taught me, it's how to laugh in the face of adversity). There are many people to meet and adventures to discover. I needed an accident to remind me it was time to start living. All you need to do is turn the page.

Robin Esrock
Vancouver, B.C.

USING THIS BOOK

You will notice this book includes little information about prices, where to stay, where to eat, the best time to go and what you should pack. Important stuff certainly, but practicalities that shift and change with far more regularity than print editions of a book. With this in mind, I've created online and social media channels to accompany the inspirational guide you hold in your hands. Here you will find all the information noted above, along with videos, galleries, reading guides and more.

By visiting www.canadianbucketlist.com, you can also join our community of bucket listers, find exclusive discounts for many of the activities discussed in this book, win prizes, and debate the merits of these and other experiences. When you register, unlock the entire site by entering the code **BUCK3TL15T**, or access each item individually with the **START HERE** link at the end of each chapter.

DISCLAIMER

Tourism is a constantly changing business. Hotels may change names, restaurants may change owners and some activities may no longer be available at all. Records fall and facts shift. While the utmost care has been taken to ensure the information provided is accurate, the author and publisher take no responsibility for errors, or for any incidents that might occur in your pursuit of these activities.

NEW BRUNSWICK

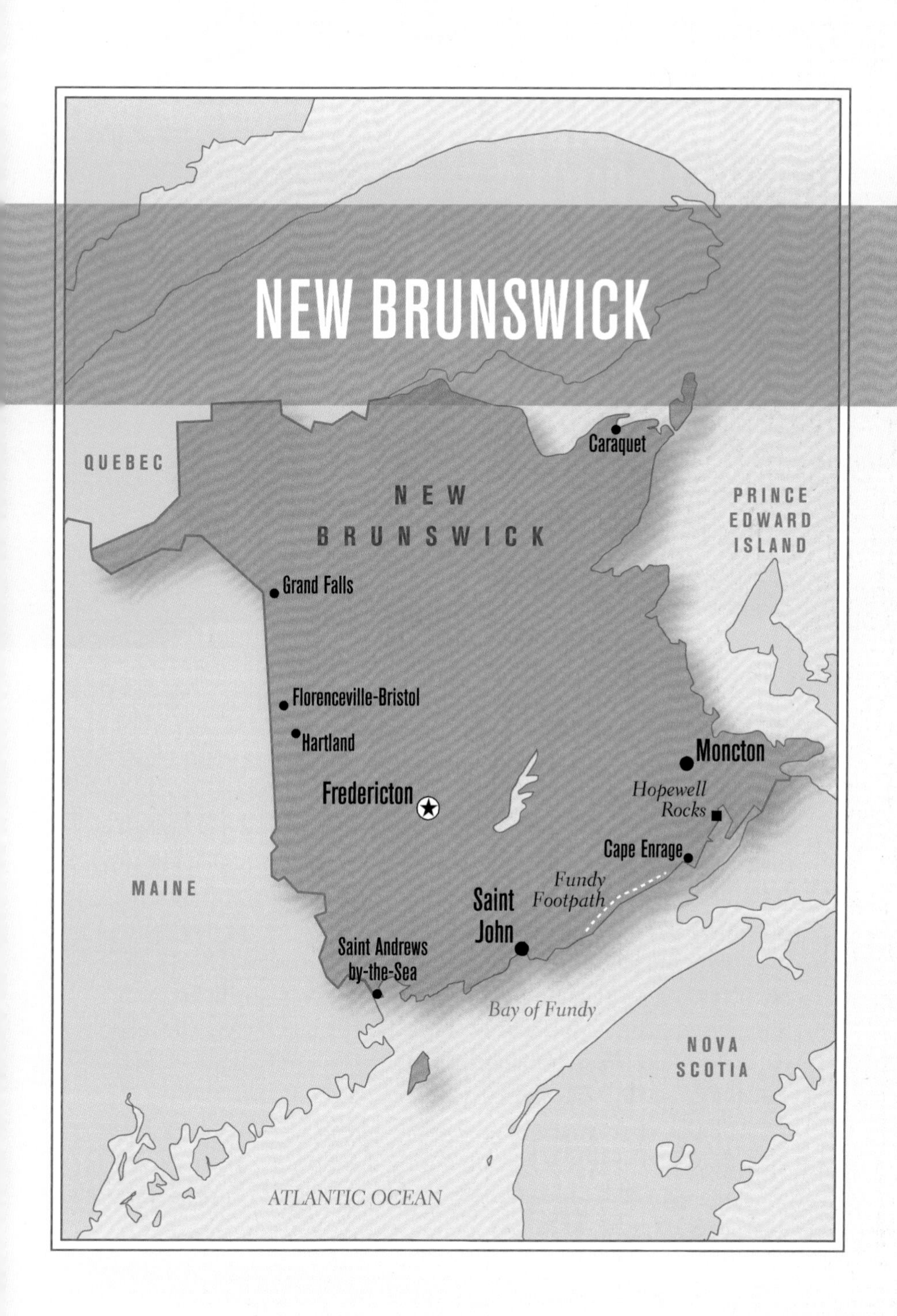

WALK THE SEABED BENEATH HOPEWELL ROCKS

Despite its contribution to my surname, geology has never rocked my casbah. It would have to be spectacular, like the fairy chimneys that poke the sky of Cappadocia, Turkey, the bizarre hoodoos at the Yehliu Geopark in Taiwan, or the basalt columns that explode out of the ground in Iceland. Point is, if it's not a mind-blowing natural phenomenon, chances are I'll take a picture and do what too many tourists do in New Brunswick: floor it for the next province. This is my headspace when I arrive at the Hopewell Rocks, the most trafficked attraction in New Brunswick. I buy my ticket, walk through an information centre, and meet a site interpreter, who, like all great guides, demonstrates that enthusiasm is infectious — even when it comes to rocks and tides.

Millions of years ago, a geological shift in tectonic plates produced a valley that was flooded during the last ice age, creating a shallow ocean floor for 100 million tons of water to rush in with the tides, rising up to sixteen metres on the shoreline. The Bay of

Fundy holds the distinction of having the world's biggest tides. New Brunswickers love this unique feature of their province (shared with Nova Scotia), and just about everyone I meet is compelled to describe the tidal phenomenon, which is why I've almost certainly explained it incorrectly. My guide reveals that during low tide we can literally walk on the ocean floor, among giant rock structures that have been carved and shaped by this daily flush of water. These are the Hopewell Rocks, which didn't excite my imagination until I saw them.

All my travels and experiences have tuned me in to the joy of discovering something truly remarkable, something you just can't see anywhere else. We walk down a metal staircase and find huge brown monoliths, shaped and squeezed like plumber's putty. Among them are natural arches, tunnels, coves, and corridors. One section feels as if I'm walking through a giant keyhole, and with green brush on top of the rocks, they do indeed look like flowerpots. The ground

Kayak the Rocks

Half the fun is paddling on tides that rise and fall the height of a five-storey building. The other half is paddling along — and sometimes directly through — the striking flowerpots and rock formations that earlier you might have walked right up to. This unique sea kayaking adventure is neither strenuous nor particularly challenging, and therefore a perfect experience for just about everybody's bucket list. ➤

is muddy and spotted with seaweed, made all the more fascinating by the fact that twice a day the very spot where I'm standing will sit more than a dozen metres underwater. Rocks have been christened with names such as Dinosaur, Lovers Arch, Mother-in-Law, and ET. More creatively, Mi'kmaq legend holds that whales in the bay once imprisoned some people. One day they tried to escape but didn't make it to shore quickly enough and were turned to stone. Now these giant sedimentary and sandstone pillars guard the coast, staring across the bay at the shores of Nova Scotia. Shorebirds fly overhead as our guide points out a nest to the delight of some international birdwatchers. Blue skies and sun would be great, but Fundy's damp mist and fog add to the otherworldliness of this strange landscape.

The tide comes in pretty quickly, so we return to the entrance, hopping over pools of water, grateful for our waterproof shoes. Later that day, this influx of water will result in a dramatically different experience, which is why many visitors consult online tide tables to ensure they catch both low and high tides. You can also hire kayaks and paddle between the flowerpots during high tide.

Having amazed a weary travel writer with no interest in geology in the first place, the Hopewell Rocks are an easy addition to our Atlantic Canada Bucket List.

START HERE: canadianbucketlist.com/hopewell

JET-BOAT THE REVERSING FALLS

Saint John is the largest city in New Brunswick — not to be confused with St. John's, Newfoundland, for one letter and an apostrophe doth a difference make. Saint John is the oldest incorporated city in Canada, the centre of industry for the Maritime provinces. Sitting on the north shore of the Bay of Fundy and at the mouth of the Saint John River, it gave us Hollywood mogul Louis B. Mayer and actor Donald Sutherland. History lesson over, let's talk about New Zealand.

You see, New Zealand has become the self-proclaimed Adrenalin Destination of the World. They've pioneered commercial thrill-seeking activities such as bungee jumping, canyon swinging, sledging, zorbing, lugeing, swooping, and skyjumping. I've done them all, twice, and can testify that, yes, you might soil your shorts in the name of fun. The point being: one must expect, and budget for, some pretty wild times when you visit New Zealand.

So how does the world's most thrilling jet boat ride — jet boats having been invented in New Zealand — end up in Saint John, New Brunswick? This thought stewed in my brain for exactly 3.6 seconds before pilot Harry Cox steered us into yet another Class 5 rapid.

In the 1950s, an industrious Kiwi farmer figured out a way to canvas the shallow waterways of his farm by inventing a high-powered boat that could zoom along in just inches of water. Jet boats, typically using powerful car engines, suck in water as a means of propulsion. Available around the world, today's boats can have the acceleration of an F-16 fighter jet. Jet boats can turn on a penny — called the Hamilton Turn after the inventor, William Hamilton — and stop on a dime. It's big business in New Zealand, where I've taken rides on the world's fastest commercial jet boat (100 kph in 4.5 seconds), jet-boated to *Lord of the Rings* locations, and bulleted through dramatic canyons near Queenstown.

How to Execute a Hamilton Turn

1. Make sure you're clear of other boats, obstructions, or nagging parents, and accelerate the engine to pick up serious speed.
2. Turn the wheel sharply in either direction, making sure you're holding on tight.
3. Cut the engine, causing the back of the boat to tilt up, spin around, and blast a huge amount of water directly onto your passengers. ➤

Very impressive, New Zealand, but you know what you don't have? The Bay of Fundy tides, backing up into the Saint John River, creating consistent Class 5 rapids without the hazard of rocks. You also don't have a pilot like Harry Cox, who over the course of twenty years' kayaking among this natural phenomenon has come to know every whirlpool, swell and drop.

Located at Fallsview Park, the jet boats operate throughout the summer, and yes, you will get wet. Bring a bathing suit and towel, leave everything in the lockers, and show up for the two hours of low tide, when the Reversing Falls is at its wildest. Among the thrill-seekers in this specially designed jet boat were two grannies and a fourteen-year-old girl. Yes, even you can do this!

The Bay of Fundy tide rises nearly eight metres in Saint John, and during low tide the waters of the 725-kilometre-long Saint John River empty into the bay, crashing through a narrow gorge and into an underwater ledge located adjacent to Fallsview Park. While you can take more genteel, scenic boat rides at other times of the day, now is the time to hop aboard Harry Cox's jet boat for what I can honestly call the ride of a lifetime. During the twenty-minute outing, the boat crests waves à la *Perfect Storm*. It slams into dips and gets spun in circles around whirlpools. Cox, laughing like the Mad

Hatter, guns the boat toward the rocky bank before slamming on the brakes, knowing full well his boat can stop in a heartbeat. He executes Hamilton Turns that drench us in the cold, brackish water of the bay, but everyone (including the grannies) is too busy screaming, laughing, and holding on to care. During brief pauses, Cox explains how the river and jet boat work, pointing out some seals, giggling like a maniac. Here is a man who clearly enjoys his job.

Back on land, knees shaking, I know without question that despite New Zealand's best efforts, little ol' New Brunswick offers the world's wildest jet boat ride.

START HERE: canadianbucketlist.com/jetboat

ABSEIL CAPE ENRAGE

The road bends and curls on the way to Cape Enrage. By its very name, you can tell this is not the Cape of Good Hope, or Cape Cod, Cape Town, or Cape Point. We're talking about fifty-metre-high cliffs that slant their eyes and glare over the Bay of Fundy. Not angry, peeved, or slightly annoyed. No, these cliffs are *enraged*, with a black heart and a permanent scowl. Acadian sailors christened the cape for its exceptionally turbulent waters, boiling at half tide above a reef stretching into the bay.

I arrive on a foggy summer morning, the atmosphere one of moody petulance. Maybe I woke up on the wrong side of the Maritimes, but the terrible weather is enough to make me throw myself off a cliff, and fortunately, that's exactly what I've come here to do.

Since 1838, Cape Enrage has had a lighthouse to warn ships during the thick fog and harsh winter storms — although that didn't stop ships from wrecking themselves on the reef all the same. When

lighthouses were automated in the 1980s, the few battered buildings that stood at Cape Enrage were scheduled for demolition until a group of Moncton schoolteachers decided to take matters into their own hands. They've worked hard to restore the remaining buildings, creating a non-profit interpretive centre and a commercial business offering kayaking, ziplining, climbing, and rappelling (or abseiling). It's mostly run by teachers and students, and despite the ominous natural surroundings, it's full of sunny Maritime dispositions.

Today I've decided to rappel off the cliff to the bottom, where I plan to hike along the beach, mindful of falling rocks and "tidal miscalculation," which can result in something unfortunate like, say, "drowning." After I slip on a harness and sit through the safety demonstration, it's a short walk over to the platform. Here's what I've learned about rappelling off a cliff: it's a lot more fun than hiking up it. It's also imperative that the, em . . . family jewels are, how should

we say, safely locked up. Fortunately, rappelling is not nearly as scary as other methods of launching oneself off a New Brunswick cliff (Walk Off a Cliff, page 22), partly because you don't have to look down. You don't want to look up too much either, since heavy falling rocks are your biggest danger.

I kick off from the sheer rock face and slowly descend to the bottom, stopping for a while to swivel around and gaze upon the furious view of the Bay of Fundy, with the shadowy shores of Nova Scotia in the distance. It doesn't take long before I'm on the beach, the cracked stone of fallen rocks all around me. The tide is coming in, so I don't stick around too long before climbing the much-appreciated metal staircase to the top. Here, an excellent restaurant rewards visitors with locally sourced dishes such as Raging Chowder and Lobster Tacos. By the time I leave, the sun even sneaks a smile from behind the clouds.

Quenched in both the adventure and culinary departments, I depart with the satisfaction of having tamed Cape Enrage, another item deserving of its place on our Atlantic Canada Bucket List.

START HERE: canadianbucketlist.com/enrage

ROLL UP MAGNETIC HILL

If I told you there was a mysterious hill outside of Moncton where you can put your car in neutral and it will roll *uphill*, would you believe me? Magnetic Hill has been one of New Brunswick's most popular attractions since the 1930s, a freak of nature that boggles the mind. Once part of the provincial highway, the mile-long anti-gravity stretch in question was preserved and today is a quirky roadside attraction adjacent to a popular water park and the largest zoo in Atlantic Canada. I admit I had my doubts when I paid the five bucks and drove to the bottom of the hill. Yet no sooner had I put the rental car in neutral than, slap-me-with-a-wet-cod, the damn wheels started rolling upward. The illusion is caused by the unusual contours of the surrounding landscape and the lack of a horizon, giving the impression that the car is rolling uphill — as if pulled toward a magnet — when in fact it is rolling downhill. It is called a gravity hill, and there are nearly a dozen of them in Canada alone, Magnetic Hill being the most famous. Isaac Newton may still be resting easy in his grave, but all the science in the world can't wipe away the wonderfully cool feeling that you're actually sliding uphill.

START HERE: canadianbucketlist.com/magnetichill

BIKE IN A KILT

There are several go-to words for travel writers that make me cringe: *Charming. Spectacular. Nestled.* I say this because I use those words all the time, and so it pains me to write that St. Andrews is a charming coastal town nestled among spectacular surroundings. And yet that's the truth, and there's no getting away from it.

Canada's first seaside resort community inspires memories of youth and genteel innocence. It's a place where people politely greet one another at the candy shoppe. It doesn't take a day before I'm on a first-name basis with a half-dozen locals, drinking a cold beer on the sun-baked patio of the Red Herring. I've written many times that travel is as much about the people you meet as the places you go, and this held true when two gentlemen greeted me in kilts at the wharf upon my return from a whale-watching excursion on the Bay of Fundy. The minke, humpbacks, finbacks, and endangered northern right whales gather in abundance in the bay, giving you a 95 percent

Canada's Small-Town Gems

If you like the small-town charm of St. Andrews, you'll enjoy visiting the following:

1. Nelson, BC
2. Legal, AB
3. Forget, SK
4. Flin Flon, MB
5. Port Hope, ON
6. Hudson, QC
7. Victoria-by-the-Sea, PEI
8. Mahone Bay, NS
9. Trinity, NL
10. Dawson, YK
11. Rankin Inlet, NU
12. Fort Smith, NT ➤

chance of encountering them on a 200-horsepower Zodiac operated by Fundy Tide Runners. Today, however, belonged to the other 5 percent, so these men in kilts were just the sort of silliness I needed to cheer me up.

Off Kilter Bike's Kurt Gumushel doesn't claim to be an ambassador for the village, or for New Brunswick in general; he just is. Considering his pedigree, it's no surprise then that Kurt likes riding his mountain bike in a kilt, and through his bike company he shares this peculiarity with tourists throughout the summer.

We bike through tall wildflowers along the coast, into a lush forest, across the rail tracks, and onto beaches of pebble. All the while I'm regaled with stories about the town, how its 1,500 population swells in the summer months, how the famed Tudor-style Algonquin Hotel wasn't actually the inspiration for Stephen King's

The Shining though that doesn't stop everyone from thinking so. It's easy to click with locals in New Brunswick, especially when you're riding through gorgeous scenery in kilts and the ride ends up at the Red Herring pub.

The rejuvenating drink of choice here in St. Andrews is a Dooryard Organic Ale, a local beer served with an orange wedge. On the patio is Kurt's dad, along with some welcoming friends, and right then and there I decide I too would like to have grown up in St.-Andrews-By-the-Sea. How peaceful to have walked among the original heritage houses barged in from Maine during the Revolutionary War, bought candy at a nineteenth-century corner shop, and practised my swing on the impossibly smooth fairways adjacent to the Algonquin. I could study marine science at the newly refurbished Huntsman Aquarium and Science Centre, and volunteer to keep the manicured Kingsbrae Gardens in tip-top shape. Who wouldn't want to live in a charming town nestled among spectacular surroundings, chomping fresh lobster rolls and slaking back Dooryards in the summer? Of course, my air-brushed dream negates those long, cold Maritime winters, which we'll conveniently overlook as we continue our journey along the Atlantic Canada Bucket List.

START HERE: canadianbucketlist.com/standrews

APPRECIATE THE GENIUS OF DALI

Art galleries need the right environment, ambience and lighting to breathe. More life can be added with the help of a knowledgeable guide — someone to explain the nuances, the deftness of meaning, the symbolism behind the strokes. All this comes together as I stand before Salvador Dali's *Santiago El Grande* in the entrance hall of Fredericton's Beaverbrook Art Gallery.

The Beaverbrook serves as the province's official art gallery, a gift from press baron Max Aitken, a.k.a. Lord Beaverbrook. Ontario-born Aitken grew up in Newcastle, New Brunswick, and went on to become a British peer and Fleet Street's first overlord, taking the name Beaverbrook to convey his Canadian roots. As a benefactor in later life, he bestowed handsome gifts on his adopted Fredericton, including the luxury hotel that bears his name, which stands right next to the art gallery.

It is here that I meet local gallery docent and professional storyteller Joan Meade. She sizes me up quickly, in tune with my belief that art without meaning is a food without taste. I've sleepwalked through many an art museum around the world, lullabyed by the monotone voice of a bored guide on a still-life audiotape. "Here is our signature piece," says Joan. The museum's icon, taking up a significant section of its gallery allotment, is quite impossible to ignore.

Dali painted his tribute to the Apostle Saint James the Great, patron saint of Spain, for the 1958 Brussels World Fair. The four-metre by three-metre canvas depicts the saint on a noble white horse, its forelegs bucking over a liquid blue ocean, with the ascension of Christ in the top right corner. The painting, regarded as one of Dali's greats, is rife with symbolism. The bottom right corner shows a lady in a monkish robe, a portrait of Dali's wife Gala, who is often present in his works. It is said that she looks at the viewer to see how the painting is being assessed. The horse's neck muscles repeat in the sky, taking the form of angels, the hidden images that are another of Dali's trademarks.

Given the horse's pose, its penis should be quite prominent in the painting. Dali has covered it with an atomic cloud, and the purest of all flowers: the jasmine. "He proclaimed that further growth of atomic power should be used for good and not for the making of bombs," explains Joan, revealing Dali's new-found interest in nuclear physics and his expression of the relationship between religion and science. Her explanation is far more interesting than my initial conclusion: that Dali covered the horse's dong with a cloud. Joan points out other

symbols. The scallop shell, Santiago el Grande's religious icon, can be seen on the horse's neck, as well as a protective shell over the saint and the coastline, which resembles the land where Dali grew up.

The painting was a gift of New Brunswick–born industrialist James Dunn, one of Beaverbrook's pals, and is on permanent display in the museum. The Dunns were early supporters and friends of Dali, and they purchased the painting under the noses of the Spanish government after the World Fair. There are several other Dali works in the museum, including portraits of the Dunns themselves. Not long after James died, and keeping it all in the family, his widow married Lord Beaverbrook. Passion! Betrayal! Oil on canvas!

Joan leads me through some of the gallery's other masterpieces: the Magritte, the Turner, the haunting Lucien Freud. She knows how to tease the life out of a painting, adding fresh colour to the canvas with her words. "A pity you're not there whenever I enter an art gallery," I tell her.

"I could be, if you're buying," she says in a snap.

Art culture in Canada tends to concentrate in the major urban centres: the National Gallery in Ottawa, the Montreal Museum of Fine Art, the Art Gallery of Ontario. Here in Fredericton, up the road from the Old Garrison District and across the street from the impressive Legislature Buildings, local character fuses with world-renowned genius for an experience even non-arty types will appreciate.

START HERE: canadianbucketlist.com/dali

Deferring to the Genius of Dali

"There are some days when I think I'm going to die from an overdose of satisfaction." – Salvador Dali ➤

WALK OFF A CLIFF

I am finally ready to step off a forty-one-metre-high cliff. While I've rappelled down gorges, caves and mountains around the world, this will be the first time I'm rappelling face first, clutching a safety rope to my belly, literally walking down a rock face. This is what one does at Open Sky Adventures, the first commercial deepelling operation on the continent. Deepelling is not bungee jumping, with its quick, what-the-hell-just-happened rush. Neither is it abseiling, where you face the wall and bounce along to the bottom. No, this is a controlled upright descent, with your eyes staring directly at sharp rocks waiting to splatter you over the riverbed. Something funny happens when I'm asked to slowly walk upright off the cliff. My mind refuses to co-operate, but my feet take the first step anyway.

The Australian army developed deepelling (also known as Aussie-style rappelling, or rap jumping) as a technique to prevent its soldiers

For Those Who'd Prefer to Jump

Deepelling requires a special sort of thrill-seeking resolve. For those who'd prefer to just jump out a plane and be done with it, check out Skydive Moncton, or the Atlantic School of Skydiving, located in Annapolis Valley, Nova Scotia. ➤

being shot while exiting helicopters. Using one hand to control the descent, it not only allowed soldiers to see their enemies, it also kept one hand free to fire back. With practice, you can literally leap off a wall like Spiderman. That practice includes repressing your natural instinct, which will beg, bargain, and plead for you to back away from the edge.

Raymond Paquet's Open Sky Adventures has been running kayak, pontoon, and canoe adventures down the Saint John River for years. When Raymond came across thrill-seekers deepelling in Quebec, he thought it would be a perfect activity for the canyon he owns just a few miles outside Grand Falls. "Babies are born afraid of height," he tells me, tightening up my mountain-climbing harness. "My job is simply to help kids get rid of this fear." His youngest client was seven, his oldest eighty, so naturally he's referring to kids of all ages.

The weight of the rope tugs me forward. Raymond has my safety line and can control my fall should I release the rope by mistake. I hold it tight to my stomach, creating a natural lock. To hop down a few metres, all I have to do is release my grip. "You've done many things in the world, Robin, but I promise you'll remember this one," says Raymond behind me.

It's always the first step. Then the second. Actually, the third is just as nerve-wracking. Halfway down, it occurs to me I'm walking at a ninety-degree angle down a cliff face. Sweat doesn't drip down my forehead, it drips right off it, splashing the ground below. Bending my knees, I launch myself off the rocks and glide several metres in a single hop, like a horizontal walk in zero gravity. Less than a minute later I reach the bottom, where I tug hard on the rope, straighten myself up, and land softly on my feet. Like all the best adrenalin activities, it's over too soon, and not soon enough.

Fortunately, the price of admission includes three jumps. I walk up the stairs to the viewing platform (easily the most strenuous part of the day), back along the road, and return to the wooden launch platform. Raymond is waiting there with a gleam in his eye. "Isn't that cool?" he says in his thick French-Canadian accent.

"I've never seen or done anything like it. Let's do it again!" I reply, and head back to the edge. It's still a mind killer taking that first step, but this time my jumps become higher and my grip becomes easier on the rope. I make my way down in a matter of seconds, whooping the whole way.

Deepelling has proved so popular that Open Sky also allows you to launch yourself off the walls of its 15-metre-high headquarters, and in all seasons, too. It was developed by the military, so it's not surprising that there's one enemy you can expect to face: the fear in your mind.

START HERE: canadianbucketlist.com/deepelling

CROSS HARTLAND'S COVERED BRIDGE

Before you enter the world's longest covered bridge, they say you should make a wish, close your eyes, cross your fingers, and hold your breath. It's no easy task making it all the way to the other side in this condition. For one thing, the bridge is 390 metres long. Second, if you're driving, you'll probably end up plummeting into the Saint John River beneath you. Chances are your wish isn't going to come true anyway, although many a young man in the early twentieth century still got lucky.

New Brunswick has sixty-one covered bridges, which provided a safe river covering, and an opportunistic spot to escape the invasive eyes of chaperones and parents. For this reason, covered bridges became known as Kissing Bridges, makeshift wooden darkrooms for

Pond Hockey Championships

If hockey is a religion in Canada, the world's largest pond hockey tournament makes the village of Plaster Rock a bucket list pilgrimage. One hundred and twenty teams from around the planet compete during the four-day event, playing hockey in its purest form — outside, on ice, surrounded by die-hard fans of the game. This is four-on-four play with no goalies or age categories on the twenty rinks built onto the frozen Roulstan Lake. It might get competitive on the ice, but the festivities continue long after the final whistle has blown in this friendly Maritime celebration. Say five "He shoots, he scores!" and all is forgiven.

START HERE: www.canadianbucketlist.com/worldpondhockey

physical romance to finally see the light. Once the horse and buggy reached the other end, scandalous passion would be left behind. I wonder if there's a generation of New Brunswickers who still get turned on by the smell of wood, the creak of floorboards, and the peculiar light that beams from the end of a tunnel.

Inside the Hartland Tunnel, my rental car robbed me of the full sensory experience, and my dad, the only other passenger in the vehicle, stole my romantic opportunity as well. Unveiled in 1901, the bridge is still the pride of Hartland, and cars line up on either side of its single-lane entries for the chance to pass through. We cross at a reasonable speed, although I'm sure farm boys slowed their

horses as much as possible. Perhaps that's why the townsfolk were so scandalized: they kept hearing "Whoa! Whoa! Whoa!" from the dark depths of the bridge. Sermons once preached the moral decay accompanying such a long covered bridge, a situation which was not helped by rumours that young men had trained their horses to stop in the middle of the bridge for the ultimate smooch spot. Sneaking a snog inside Hartland's covered bridge is a long-standing Canadian tradition. If it's just you and a family member, though, it's perfectly acceptable to grunt and say: "Cool bridge."

START HERE: canadianbucketlist.com/hartland

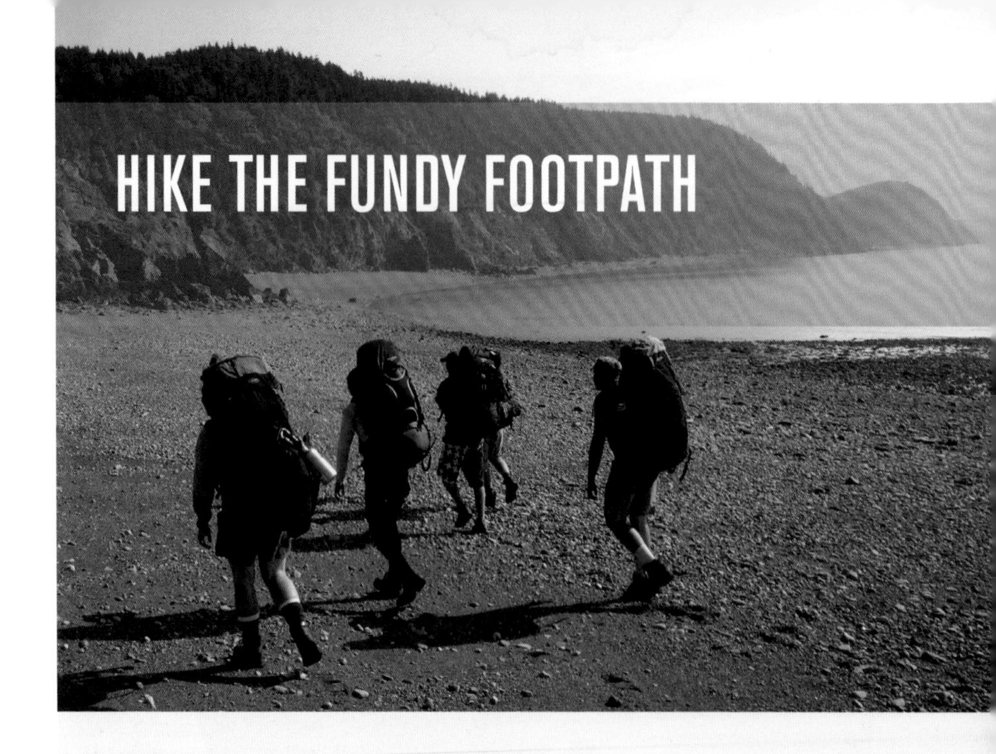

HIKE THE FUNDY FOOTPATH

Much like Vancouver Island's West Coast Trail, this forty-one-kilometre multi-day adventure tests hikers with its wild conditions and challenging backcountry terrain. Tracing the Bay of Fundy coastline, the footpath begins at the suspension bridge at Big Salmon River and concludes in Goose River, which can only be crossed during low tide. Immersed in the microclimate of the Bay of Fundy, you'll be exploring the Maritime Acadian Highlands, part of the foothills of the Appalachian mountain range. That's a fancy way of saying you'll be knee-deep in fog, steep river valleys, and strenuous switchback trails ready to spook the average day hiker. Trekking alongside one-hundred-metre cliffs, through old-growth forests, beaches, and streams, the footpath provides a true test for your backcountry wilderness skills. After a half-dozen emergency evacuations one year, volunteers who maintain the trail issued a warning that the footpath is too rugged for novice hikers. That rules me out, but adventurous, experienced hikers will definitely want to add this to their bucket lists.

Budget 4-5 days, and keep your tide chart handy.

START HERE: canadianbucketlist.com/fundyfootpath

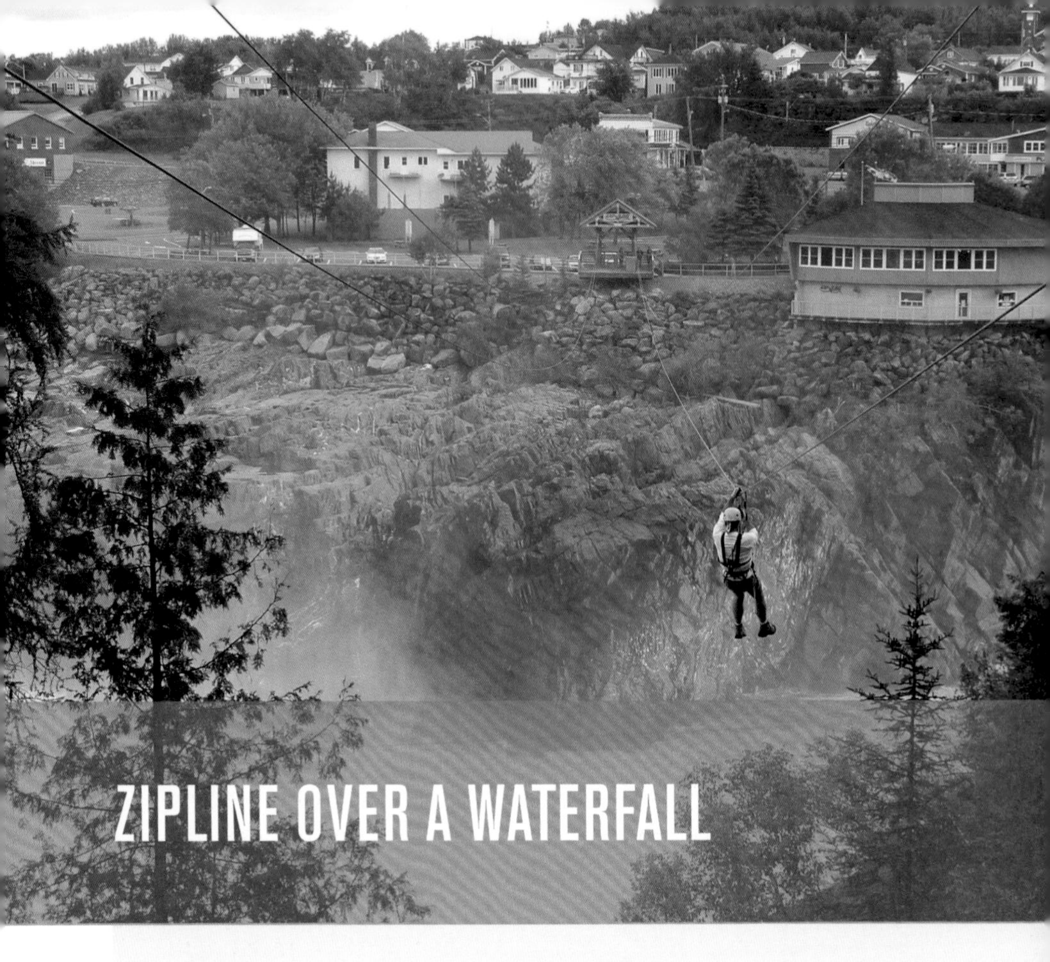

ZIPLINE OVER A WATERFALL

Before invading just about every jungle block in Costa Rica, ziplines were a practical necessity in mountainous regions, where they were a means of transporting both goods and people. With the boom in ecotourism, enterprising operators realized tourists will pay good money for the opportunity to slide faster than monkeys through the canopy, learning about the environment as they do so. I've ziplined on four continents, and here's what I've come to realize:

1. Anyone can zipline.
2. Ziplining is only as good as the environment in which you do it.

Usually, the environment consists of trees, which is why this neat little operation in Grand Falls zipzags its way onto the bucket list.

Where to Zipline in Atlantic Canada:

1. **Anchors Above Zipline**, Pictou County, NS
2. **North Atlantic Ziplines**, Petty Harbour, NL
3. **Cape Enrage**, NB
4. **Marble Zip Tours**, Steady Brook, NL
5. **TreeGo**, Moncton or Mactaquac, NB. ➤

The town is named after the waterfalls it cradles, where the Saint John River drops twenty-three metres over a rock ledge, creating one of the largest Canadian falls east of Niagara. Eric Ouellette, a local civil engineer with some big industrial projects under his belt, saw the potential and opened Zip Zag for business. It took his team two years to build dual racing ziplines across the gorge, spanning 150 metres above the raging whitewater. He rightly believed that the only thing sweeter than a huge waterfall is ziplining through its spray on a bright, sunny day.

I collect my harness at the Malabeam Information Centre, where visitors learn about the area's history, the hydroelectric project, and how Eric and his team used 2,500 ice blocks to create the world's largest domed igloo, as certified by Guinness World Records. Clearly, here is an impressive man committed to random achievements. The only requirements for zipzaggers are that they weigh between 25 kilos and 125 kilos and are capable of walking up stairs.

Eric's wife, Christine, slips me into a harness and gives a brief demonstration, and then we walk to the launch zipline. Ziplining is perhaps the easiest of all "adrenalin" activities, requiring hardly any physical effort, and offering the security of knowing you're safely connected to a steel rope over-engineered to take the weight of an elephant. Once I kick off, it takes only seconds to get across the canyon, which is where the real fun begins: the dual lines twenty-three metres above the waterfalls.

Grand Falls, also known as Grand Sault, is one of only two municipalities in Canada with a bilingual name. Over 80 percent

of its population are completely bilingual, including all the Zip Zag guides. This is useful for American customers (the town is right on the Maine border) and Québécois customers driving in from eighty kilometres away. Regardless of whether you whoop in French or in English, once your feet leave the wooden platform, you'll find yourself gliding along at thirty to forty kilometres an hour, and with an awfully big smile on your face. A sheet of fine mist gently sprays me as I make the crossing, which is over too soon, as ziplines usually are. While the overall experience might take around an hour, the actual flying time can be counted in seconds. But believe me, those seconds count infinitely more when you're flying over a raging waterfall as opposed to a jungle canopy. There's no practical reason why anyone needs to zipline in this day and age, which is exactly why it's so much fun to do so.

START HERE: canadianbucketlist.com/zipline

PAINT YOUR FACE AT TINTAMARRE

It's August 15, and the descendants of Acadia are eager to make some noise. When the church bells toll 6:00 p.m., tens of thousands of people erupt onto the streets of Caraquet dressed in costumes, making a right French-Canadian racket with whatever they can get their hands on: drums, bells, horns, buckets, whistles, voices. The annual tintamarre (literally, "clangour") tradition in Caraquet is remarkable for a number of reasons. First, the population of this seaside town is just over four thousand — so where did the other thirty-four thousand people come from? Second, the tradition of celebrating Acadian culture and history with tintamarre only dates back to 1979. By the enthusiasm on display, one would think it was part of the three-hundred-year-old Acadian heritage. Third, it's just about the most fun you can have in New Brunswick, with or without the face paint.

Origins of Acadia

Once a distinct and separate colony of New France, Acadia was named after a Greek district, the word meaning "place of refuge." Given the brutal deportation of Acadians by the British in the 1750s, it turned out to be everything but. Queen Elizabeth II issued a royal apology for the eviction in 2003. ➤

The story of Acadia, with its origins in seventeenth- and eighteenth-century French settlement in the Maritimes, is a tumultuous one. Wars, displacement, deportation, and cultural invasion — it's a wonder any culture has survived at all. In 1955, the Church organized a celebration in Moncton to commemorate the two-hundredth anniversary of the Acadian Deportation, when conquering British armies dispersed the population. The racket that ensued left a lasting impression, although it wasn't until 1979 that tintamarre resurfaced as a massive street festival in the town of Caraquet. The town already boasts an Acadian Historical Village and Acadian summer festival, so it was the perfect place to celebrate the 375th anniversary of Acadia's founding. Acadia, I should point out, was a part of New France that included much of the Maritimes and parts of Maine. Acadians who resettled in Louisiana became known as Cajuns.

Back to 1979: everyone in Caraquet was invited to participate in the parade, embrace the tricolour Acadian flag, and delight in a doozy of decibels. Although it was supposed to be a one-off event, a year later folks emerged from their houses with pots, pans, barrels, and sticks. Soon after, costumes and face paint had been added, and visitors were flocking in from all over the province. Community leaders were already talking about holding a "traditional" tintamarre, despite the fact the tradition had barely begun to exist. Today, tintamarre has evolved into a vital expression of Acadian history, culture, and pride. It has spread to other Acadian communities in New Brunswick and to parts of Quebec, a symbol of Acadian identity.

But wait a second, Robin. We're not Acadian, so why should we care?

I'll explain as I paint your face in red, white, and blue, with a golden star around your right eye.

For a start, where else can you make more noise than the kids and be admired for it? Embracing the festival's joie de vivre is the kind of fun few should turn down. Unlike Fat Tuesday, this carnival makes an effort to include tourists and visitors, adding everyone into the mix, inviting participation and even home invasions. Tintamarre is the climax of the two-week-long Acadian Festival, featuring hundreds of music concerts, step-dancing, art, competitions, and food. Feast on traditional Acadian fare such as *fricot à la poule*, clam pie, and pulled molasses taffy. If you're historically inclined, 80 percent of the buildings in the Acadian Village are from the 1770s to the 1890s, relocated to the re-enactment village for an authentic material reference to history.

But it's the atmosphere and the smiley side of chaos that have made tintamarre one of the biggest festivals in the Atlantic provinces. Besides the party, tintamarre is an opportunity to understand and appreciate a vital cultural element that makes Canada Canada, and not, say, Australia with snow. Make some noise, together with the descendants of the Acadians: "We're here, and we're not going anywhere!"

START HERE: canadianbucketlist.com/tintamarre

DRINK A POTATO SMOOTHIE

Welcome to the home of the world's favourite side dish. One-third of the world's frozen french fries are produced right here in Florenceville-Bristol, distributed by the McCain factory to 110 countries. If there were any justice, you would walk into a pub in Bangkok and order a burger with Canadian fries. Perhaps even New Brunswickan fries.

Named after Florence Nightingale, this small, hyphenated town in Carlton County is home to the McCain frozen food empire, which processes around a million pounds of potatoes per hour. Fittingly, the McCain family are loyal supporters of the Potato World Museum, a quirky roadside attraction dedicated to the beauty of the world's favourite tuber. I make my way past the interpretive centre, which

Traditional Food in Atlantic Canada

New to the region? Sink your teeth into:

- Newfoundland's cod tongues, brewis, Jiggs' dinner, and toutons
- Nova Scotia's lobster poutine, and hodgepodge
- PEI's Cow's Creamery ice cream, and Anne of Green Gables raspberry cordial
- New Brunswick's fiddleheads and dried dulse.

features customary wax models of farmers and horses. The Antique Machinery section leaves no doubt that harvesting potatoes is not nearly as easy as picking them up prewashed in plastic bags at the supermarket. In the interactive displays I learn that *potato* comes from the Amerindian word *batata*, and that potatoes were introduced to larger public appetites by sixteenth-century Spanish conquistadores in South America. Potatoes have been responsible for war, famine, heartache, and heartburn. They were the first food grown in space, potato blossoms have been sported as garment decorations by royalty, there are four thousand different varieties, and . . . I could go on, but there's a smell permeating from the café and it's been a half-hour since I tucked into a bag of potato chips.

I briskly walk past the Potato Hall of Recognition, which features portraits of old white guys who have been instrumental in the development of the province's potato industry. Some of them are surnamed McCain, naturally, and I can't help but notice that some of these guys have heads shaped like potatoes, too.

Potato World's café is where things really get interesting. Ever since Thomas Jefferson introduced french fries to guests at the White House in the early 1800s, the delicious domination of the deep-fried potato has been unstoppable. Can you imagine fish and rice? Well, yes, but it's not fish 'n' chips, innit? Fries are served everywhere, from the most haughty high-end restaurants to gut-swilling dives. On the other hand, Potato World's café creations are a true homage to the potato's flexibility. Their fries come in the following flavours:

Lemon and Herb, Sweet Chili Pepper, BBQ, Tex Mex, Outbacka, Chili and Cheese, and poutine, of course. Forget the ketchup and reach for the white balsamic-cayenne mayo. Indulge your sweet tooth with potato fries and chocolate sauce, or fries rolled in cinnamon and brown sugar. And wash it all down with a strawberry, banana, or wildberry potato smoothie. Yes, smoothie.

Since my visit to Florenceville-Bristol, potato chips have never tasted quite the same. No matter where I am in the world, with each bite I can close my eyes and picture the bucolic hills of New Brunswick, the old iron hoes in the museum, the flowing waters of the Saint John River, and the steam billowing out of the McCain factory. Now that's a flavour worth dipping your chips into.

START HERE: canadianbucketlist.com/potato

NOVA SCOTIA

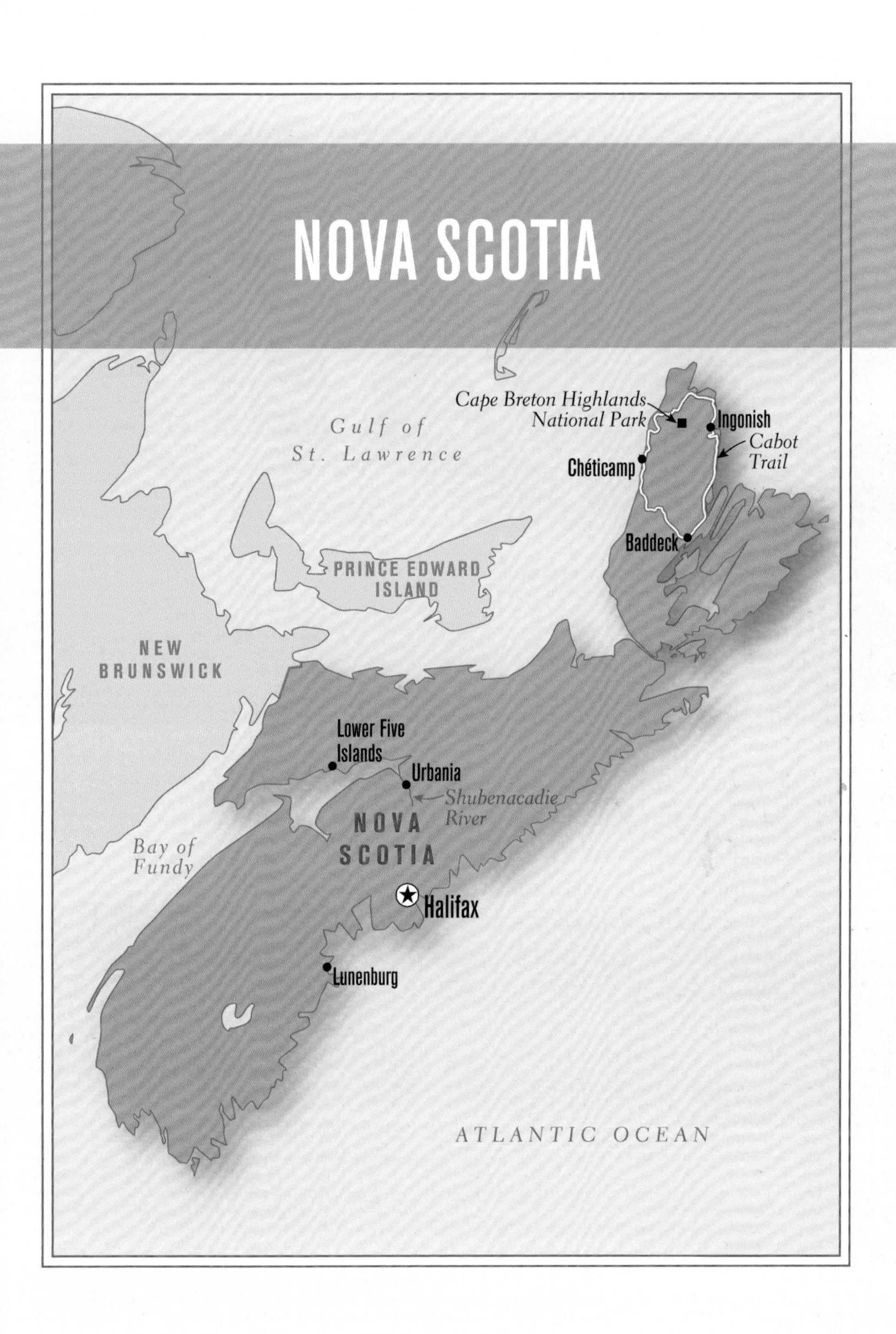

Cape Breton Highlands
National Park
Ingonish
Cabot
Trail
Chéticamp
Baddeck
Gulf of
St. Lawrence
PRINCE EDWARD
ISLAND
NEW
BRUNSWICK
Lower Five
Islands
Urbania
Shubenacadie
River
NOVA
SCOTIA
Bay of
Fundy
Halifax
Lunenburg
ATLANTIC OCEAN

RAFT A TIDAL WAVE

When Nova Scotia's largest river, the Shubenacadie, encounters the rush of tidal water flowing in from the Bay of Fundy, *bore* is not the word that comes to mind. Yet the world's largest tides, reversing into the very rivers that feed them, are called exactly that: tidal bores. It is a true tidal wave (not to be confused with a tsunami), as the leading wave swallows sandbars and marshes in a matter of minutes, leaving a turbulent trail of waves and rapids in its wake.

There are few places in the world where you can experience this phenomenon, much less hop on a high-powered Zodiac to play in it like a theme park ride. Once a day, rafting companies along the low, shallow banks of the Shube gather clients for the incoming bore, which can bring waves as high as five metres rumbling over the muddy sandbars before harmlessly levelling out.

It's a crisp June morning when I arrive at Tidal Bore Rafting's HQ. Depending on the tide and moon cycle, the bore's size can be classified as mild, medium, or extreme. I've enjoyed the thrill of Class 5 whitewater rafting before (including the world's highest commercial vertical drop in New Zealand), and so I look forward to today's extreme conditions. The seventy-two-kilometre-long river is brackish and brown, a stream of chocolate milk running through minty green forests and farmland. I'm advised not to wear anything I care too deeply about, and am handed a rainsuit, a life jacket, and a pair of old shoes.

Surf Tidal Bores

The tidal bore on New Brunswick's Petitcodiac River has also been creating waves. Two Californian surfers set a North American record, riding a single wave for twenty-nine kilometres. With hazardous rocks and rough conditions, only experienced lunatics need apply.

Our group makes its way to the riverbank, the water running calmly about six metres below the jetty. We squish over thick mud, hop into the Zodiac, and introduce ourselves. I'm with a couple from Halifax, and we're guided by a young pilot named Gillian, who swaps out as a ski instructor in the river's off-season. She pilots the Zodiac upriver, and with the high-tide line clearly marked on the riverbank way above our heads, my imagination starts to run riot. I picture a massive tidal wave, twenty metres high, rushing down the valley and drowning everything in its path, like those water horses conjured by Arwen in *The Lord of the Rings*. Gillian is less concerned, pointing out the first of many bald eagles that have gathered along the Shube in high concentrations to feed on sea and river fish caught in the tides. It's the reason the area is home to the highest nesting concentration of bald eagles on North America's east coast.

Under their watchful eagle eyes, the Zodiac hums along with the current, passing the site of a huge mudslide that took a few trees with it. We're a little early and so berth on a sandbar, eagerly awaiting the arrival of the bore, occupying our time by submerging our shins in sinking sand. Ten minutes later, Gillian points upriver. In the

distance, a harmless white wave approaches. It seems innocent enough, not nearly as extreme as I had imagined. Gillian guns the Zodiac to meet the wave, which we ramp over and then turn back, surfing on its crest. Within minutes the wave will swallow the sandbars and begin its rise to the tide line, high on the cliffs above our heads. The Zodiac pulls out, racing farther upstream. "Are you ready, guys?" Gillian yells. What she knows, and what we don't, is that as the high tide hits sandbars and slopes, the rush of water gets churned up like a boiling soup.

After zooting up the relatively calm side of the river, Gillian makes a hard left, and we drop in like unprepared potatoes. Bang! Ow! Wow! Whee! Bang! There's not much else we can say as the Zodiac dips and crests through the rapids, lurching feet in the air, landing hard with a thud. Keeping our mouths shut is actually a smart idea, as the Shube's muddy water drenches the boat, ready to spoon us with eager mouthfuls. The rapids are cold, invigorating, and relentless. When they peter out, Gillian repeats the process, skirting the soup close to the shore before turning in for another thrill ride.

Earlier, we had passed a rock formation known as Anthony's Point, which looked like a large boot sitting far above our heads. Now it is completely submerged. We hit the soup again, and again, a concentrated and sustained dose of rapids you just can't find on traditional whitewater adventures. My knees take a beating from the drops as we get pummelled from all sides, almost losing a shipmate at one point. However, with no rocks to worry about, should you lose a man overboard, it's a relatively safe affair for the boat to find you and haul you back on board. We ride the waves until the riverbanks widen and the bore wears itself out, conveniently close to the jetty we left two hours ago. I can barely recognize its wooden steps, floating above a raging river where before they sat on metres of mud.

A hot shower later, we exchange high-fives and wide smiles, proud recipients of a true Canadian adventure you just can't find anywhere else. Despite its modern usage, the word *bore* comes from Old Norse, meaning "swell" — a word that applies both literally and figuratively to this bucket list adventure.

START HERE: canadianbucketlist.com/tidalbore

STROLL AROUND LUNENBURG

Atlantic Canada's coastline is flecked with seaside fishing villages that recall another era, an age when raw dog fishermen braved rough oceans to haul in cod that would be salted and shipped to all parts of the British Empire. The exceptionally well-preserved fishing town of Lunenburg, founded in 1753, stands apart for a number of reasons. It has been designated a UNESCO World Heritage Site for being the "best surviving example of a planned British colonial settlement in North America, retaining the town's original layout and overall appearance, based on a rectangular grid pattern drawn up in the home country." I decided to visit the town to understand what that sentence means, because, let's face it, UNESCO don't make it sound very exciting.

The Legend of the *Bluenose*

Built and launched in Lunenburg, the *Bluenose* captured the world's imagination as the fastest fishing boat on the seas, holding the International Fisherman's Trophy for seventeen years. This hulking ship was a far cry from the sleek modern vessels that race in today's sailing events; it was primarily used for fishing in some of the world's stormiest waters. Immortalized in music and books, on stamps, Nova Scotia licence plates, and the Canadian dime, history finally caught up with the old boat. It was sold as a cargo ship in the Caribbean and wrecked beyond repair on a reef in Haiti. Several replicas have been built over the years for promotional and leisure purposes, with a new replica just recently completed in Lunenburg. ➤

Driving in on a fine spring day, I'm reminded of an idyllic British seaside resort, complete with busloads of tourists. High season hasn't quite kicked in yet, but the town has tidied itself up after the long winter, eager to welcome new summer guests. My first stop is the excellent Fisheries Museum of the Atlantic, which does a great job breathing life into the legacy of East Coast fishing. I learn about the birth of the industry, the fisherman's lifestyle through the years, the challenges, the science, the equipment, and the rum-runners who made their fortune during Prohibition. There is also an exhibition about the *Bluenose* — the Lunenburg legend honoured on the back of every Canadian dime. What strikes me most are the stories of clippers lost at sea, many with all crew onboard. One fierce hurricane, the August Gale of 1927, sank several ships and claimed 184 souls. A memorial lists the names of local fishermen who never returned to shore, from the 1800s all the way up to the present day. We've come a long way from fishermen using single lines to pull in cod, getting paid in cod tongues, and braving treacherous conditions.

Across the bay is High Liner Foods, one of North America's largest fish processing plants. Modern fishing has made the profession safer but has also devastated fish stocks, and with them entire communities. All this makes the museum's exhibits seem so vital to Atlantic Canada's

history. From the museum, I stroll along the waterfront, admiring the colourful paint jobs on the old wharves and wooden houses.

To get behind the charming facade, I join local guide Shelah Allen for one of her historical walking tours. Storms are threatening when we meet outside the impressive Academy building, built in 1894. The weather doesn't dampen Shelah's enthusiasm one bit, as she begins to tell me stories about the houses, what era they're from, their architecture, former inhabitants, and why they're so well preserved.

"Here's my favourite house," she says, pointing to a large pink Victorian on York Street. Built in 1888, Morash House has overhanging windows, triple bellcast roofs and a Lunenburg "bump" — large windows facing the ocean so that hopeful wives could watch for ships returning safely to port. Across the street is another old home, painted yellow. "That's actually been rebuilt pretty recently," says Shelah. The town is serious about keeping its heritage well intact. At the end of the block is the oldest Lutheran church in Canada, reflecting the many German immigrants who made Lunenburg their home.

Each wooden home we pass has a story, until we come to the striking St. John's Anglican Church, faithfully restored after a devastating

fire in 2001. An organist is playing inside, adding to the atmosphere. I learn about the many Norwegian fishermen stranded here during the Second World War and taken in by the locals, and the warm relations that still exist as a result. We wander down King Street, past the bright green and orange wooden shops that caused a little stir when the paint dried, ending up at the Knaught–Rhuland House, one of the best-preserved eighteenth-century houses in the country, and another National Historic Site.

Shelah's one-hour tour ends at the pub, because that's just how things work in Nova Scotia. She tells me that Lunenburg is growing with an influx of entrepreneurs, and that, coupled with the town's ability to preserve and showcase its history, is making the future look pretty peachy. UNESCO's description sounds terribly square — *grid, rectangular, layout*. Rest assured, there's a warm heart waiting to greet you in Lunenburg.

START HERE: canadianbucketlist.com/lunenburg

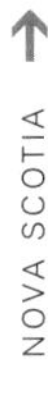

ARM A CANNON AT THE HALIFAX CITADEL

"Atten-SHUN!"

The kilted sergeant of the 78th Highlanders is doing his best to get our motley regiment into line. Granted, he's actually a paid historical re-enactor, and our regiment consists of confused tourists from Mexico, Germany, and France. Call us the rank and vile. We had signed up to be soldiers for a day at Fort George, Halifax's most iconic landmark, overlooking the city atop Citadel Hill. The year is 1869, when the red-coated and kilted Scottish Highlanders manned the fort that protected the crux of British shipping interests on the Atlantic coast. We'd each been given a shilling, which crafty sergeants dropped into the pints of young men who would soon discover they'd just signed up for a seven-year stint in Her Majesty's Army. Today we would discover what this might have been like — from barracks to guard posts — breathing fresh life into this National Historic Site.

In the mid-1700s, the British built a fort on the highest hill overlooking Halifax harbour. It continued to expand until the current

Citadel was completed in 1856, designed to be a potent deterrent to American, French, and other aggressors threatening lucrative British naval interests. With excellent sightlines, thick stone walls, powerful cannon, and even a land moat, the star-shaped fortress was so successful that it never did come under attack. Unless you count tourists, penetrating the walls daily to explore this living museum and enjoy its views of the city.

Operated by Parks Canada, the Citadel provides a snapshot of life behind the walls in 1869. Historical re-enactors run through daily chores, inviting visitors to join them through the "Soldier for a Day" program and the Halifax Citadel Experience. Which is how I came to be position number five, awaiting the order to transfer a bucket of make-believe black powder to position number three, so that position number two could pretend to stoke the very real cannon and blast non-existent enemies to smithereens. While the Citadel never came under enemy fire, it did witness the tragic Halifax Explosion. In 1917, a munitions ship exploded in the harbour, flattening nearby buildings and killing some two thousand people.

Back to the present, where, according to the cannon master, we are the worst crew he's ever seen. At least he doesn't have to hear our awfulness, unlike the drum instructor, who must listen to my version of a brass shell field drum. Picture Animal, the drummer for the Muppets. *Rat-atat-a-ratatatatata* . . . Thank you, Robin, someone else, please. Anyone?

Next is the barracks, where we learn how up to twenty men would share these spartan quarters with their families, the kids sleeping under the creaking narrow bed. When winter came, even the hardiest of Highlanders had to wear pants, taking solace in the fact they were made of Mackenzie-clan tartan. Naturally, I ask a soldier if he's a true Scotsman.

"My boots are the only item beneath my kilt," he replies. Minutes later, a gust of wind causes an embarrassing Marilyn Monroe moment, and I can confirm kilts are not nearly as becoming as white dresses.

After visiting the huge waterless moat, designed to turn attackers into sitting ducks, we learn about weapons and watch a demonstration with a working nineteenth-century muzzle. The loud crack of black powder reminds us that these high-calibre bullets would stop an elephant, and certainly ruin the day of anyone on the receiving end. For Queen and country, the soldiers might say, pulling the trigger, feeling the breeze on their knees. Still, for all its red-coated pomp and glory, it was no fun to be in Her Majesty's Army.

Today, the Citadel continues to guard the city of Halifax like a brawny, protective grandparent. It's well worth a visit, especially now, when even the soldiers are smiling.

START HERE: canadianbucketlist.com/citadel

Twin Tragedies in Halifax

The Citadel has borne witness to two of the early twentieth century's greatest tragedies. In 1910, Halifax was the closest port of call to the Titanic disaster. Plucked from the ocean, survivors were taken to New York, but the dead were routed to Halifax. The 150 victims are buried in three cemeteries across the city. Today, the Maritime Museum of the Atlantic houses an extensive collection of Titanic artifacts. By the way, the tombstone marked J. Dawson in the Fairview Cemetery has nothing to do with the Leonardo DiCaprio character in the movie (but that doesn't stop flowers appearing around it anyway).

Seven years later, an accident in the harbour resulted in the largest man-made explosion prior to the invention of the nuclear bomb. Like many disasters, it resulted from a series of unfortunate events. A Norwegian vessel collided with a French ammunition ship in the harbour's narrow strait. A fire attracted thousands of locals to the shore, and twenty minutes later, when it ignited the ammunition, the ship was blasted nearly three hundred metres into the air. More than 1,600 people were essentially vapourized, along with every building within a 2.6-kilometre radius. Nine thousand people were injured, and the death toll topped two thousand. Factor in an eighteen-metre-high tsunami and raging fires, and you can understand why the Halifax Explosion is still regarded as one of history's greatest disasters. ➤

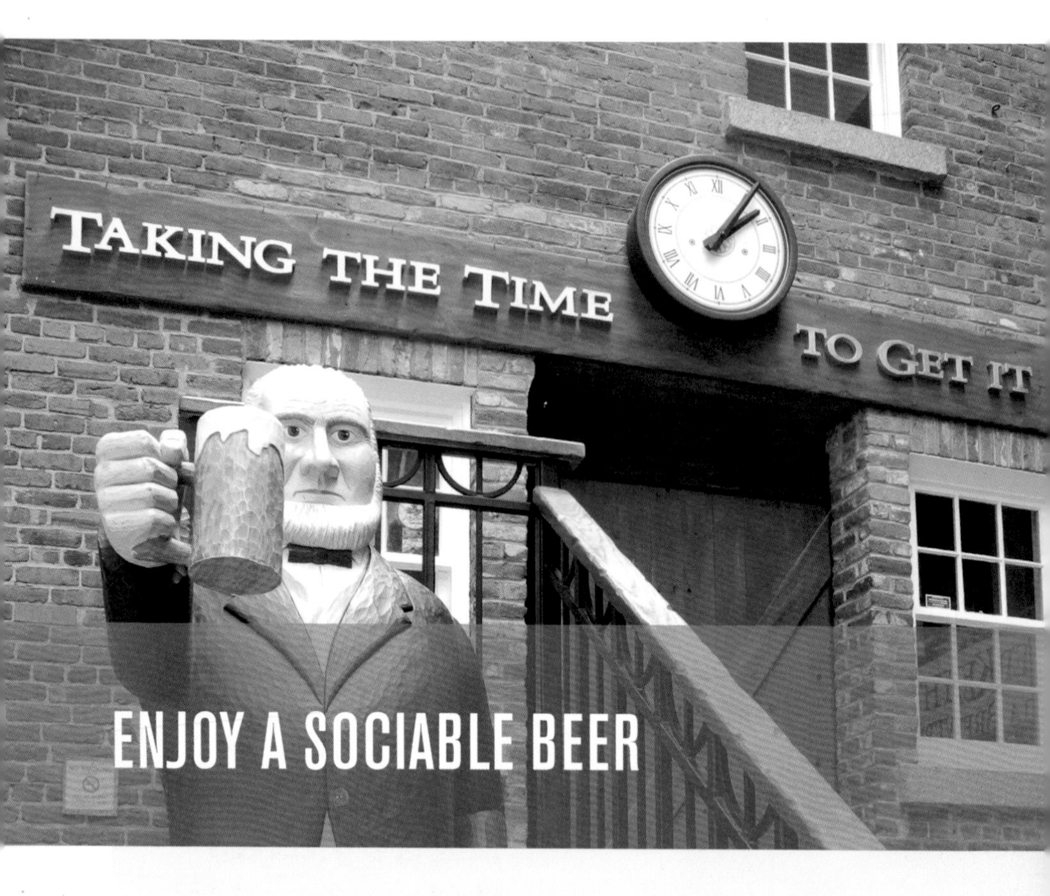

ENJOY A SOCIABLE BEER

It is my custom, on the road, always to order the local beer. The thought of ordering Heineken in Hungary, Miller in Mexico, or Corona in China may be a boon for major beer monopolies, but not for the authentic traveller. Beers taste better in the land of their brewing — except for Budweiser in the United States and Chang in Thailand, which are best enjoyed nowhere. Canada's beer, it must be said, is vastly underrated in terms of its quality. Visit Australia and you'll see how even a committed beer-drinking nation is forced to consume weak, industrial beverages such as VB, XXXX, and Tooheys. Phooey!

While microbreweries have made great-tasting inroads in North America, Down Under, and beyond, I'll take the mass-market Kokanee, Rickard's, Sleeman, Big Rock, and Moosehead over best-selling foreign brands any day. And then there is Alexander Keith's, purveyors of fine Nova Scotian beer since 1820. Although it's now

Fine Bucket List Beers of Atlantic Canada:

a.k.a. "It was a tough job researching this list, but someone had to do it."

1. **Gahan House Brewery** (PEI) Sir John A's Honey Wheat: light, quaffable, and readily available throughout the province on tap.
2. **Garrison Brewing** (NS) Sugar Moon Maple: seasonal favourite with a tang of all-natural maple syrup from the excellent Sugar Moon Farm.
3. **Quidi Vidi** (NL) Iceberg Beer: distinctive blue bottle for a crisp beer made with 25,000-year-old iceberg water.
4. **Pump House Brewery** (NB) Blueberry Ale: malts, spicy hops, with the essence and flavour of blueberries.
5. **A L'Abri de la Tempete** (QC Maritime) Belle Saison: a staple for the Maggies' award-winning microbrewery, scented with herbs harvested on the islands.
6. **Picaroons Traditional Ales** (NB) Dooryard Organic Summer Ale: blend of three wheat styles with a citrus, spicy finish.

owned by Labatt (in turn owned by Anheuser–Busch InBev, which owns just about everything else), Keith's holds a special place in the hearts of Nova Scotians. I'm told it is the largest-distributed non-specialty beer in the country, and while I'm not exactly sure what that means, it sounds as if it holds a special place in the hearts of many Canadians too.

Which explains why the Brewery Tour, held in the same brick building on Lower Water Street in which Alexander Keith created his famous Indian Pale Ale, is a popular attraction in Halifax. Historical

re-enactors walk you through the history of the man, the beer, and the city before depositing you one hour later in an old-fashioned tavern where you can enjoy the fruits of your labours. It's a little hokey, and I'm hesitant to say you must take this tour before you die, because, quite frankly, you might have more fun with your mates at the adjacent pub, the Stag's Head. Whatever pub you end up in in Nova Scotia, ordering a pint of Keith's will endear you to the locals, lubricate new friendships, and possibly turn out to be more fun than any item on this bucket list. Probably not, but what is a beer if not its potential to lead to something more, even if it is the gutter? So raise a glass to all of Canada's beautiful beers, and say, like a true Nova Scotian, "Sociable!"

START HERE: canadianbucketlist.com/beer

RUN A RACE OF BIBLICAL PROPORTIONS

We all know the Bible story: Moses leads the Israelites out of slavery in Egypt, chased by the resentful Pharaoh's army to the shores of the Red Sea. Here, Moses raises his staff and one of the great Biblical miracles occurs: the sea divides, allowing the Israelites to pass safely across the ocean floor. The pursuing army are swallowed by the sea, and lo, the Israelites are free . . . to wander the desert for forty years.

But that's another story. Now let's replace the Red Sea with the Bay of Fundy, which we already know has the world's highest tides. Instead of the Israelites racing for freedom, picture joggers covered up to their ankles in red mud. For the pursuing soldiers, we'll use Time itself, which relentlessly ticks forward until the bay begins to fill, drowning rocks and mud up to fifteen metres underwater. Not since Moses has there been a race against such a powerful foe, hence the name of this quirky and extreme ten-kilometre annual run along Five Islands, Nova Scotia, which is called . . . Not Since Moses!

Over one thousand competitors must race along the ocean floor — over mud, seaweed, rocks, muck, and slime — to reach the finish line before high tide. These conditions make it particularly treacherous, but the well-organized event takes great pride in ensuring that no one is forced to swim to safety. Participants in the ten-kilometre run, or the less frenetic five-kilometre walk, follow a path among five islands that sit off the coast: Moose, Diamond, Egg, Pinnacle, and Long. If you stop long enough to admire your surroundings (and don't slip on seaweed), you'll see eroded muddy cliffs, sandbars, and distinct islands of rock — and probably a jogger knee-deep in sludge, his or her shoes lodged firmly in the mud.

The volunteer-driven event is a festive affair, culminating in live music, hot food, a poetry reading, and a popular children's event. Run times typically fall between sixty and ninety minutes, with the winner clocking in at around forty-five minutes and the last runner at around two hours, by which stage the kids are already enjoying a burger and the annual Basket Run. Conditions can vary from year to year — strong winds once had competitors wading through a waist-high tidal river — and volunteer stations along the route are known to turn back slow runners. Fortunately, boats are on hand for rescues, since this is not a triathlon — yet. How great would it be to see a race on the ocean floor that starts on foot and finishes with a swim?

Not Since Moses benefits local schools, draws athletes from around the world and relies on the uncanny ability of Nova Scotians to, well, run with it. Besides the sticky terrain, runners are cautioned to expect strong winds and bring their own water (or alcohol, if that's the fuel you need). It may not be a Biblical miracle, but Not Since Moses still crosses the mud-splattered line to finish on the Great Atlantic Canada Bucket List.

START HERE: canadianbucketlist.com/moses

A Foodie Escape

Located alongside the Bay of Fundy, the Annapolis Valley is the third most important fruit-growing region in the country, blessed with some of the best weather in Atlantic Canada. Besides the inviting towns and seafront views, foodies will love the culinary choices on offer, particularly fine dining at boutique wineries. Wine Access magazine named Le Caveau Restaurant, located at the Domaine de Grand Pre winery, as one of the world's twenty best vineyard restaurants. Not far away is the Fox Hill Cheese House, which produces twenty types of specialty cheeses, along with yogourt and gelato. Foodies will also enjoy the Wolfville Farmer's Market, which takes place Wednesday evenings and Saturdays during the summer. The Farmer's Market also presents "Tastes of the Valley," a celebration of local food that has the region's best chefs creating locally sourced dishes. ➤

EXPLORE CAPE BRETON AND THE CABOT TRAIL

"I have travelled around the globe. I have seen the Canadian and American Rockies, the Andes, the Alps and the Highlands of Scotland, but for simple beauty, Cape Breton outrivals them all."

Thus spoke Alexander Graham Bell, the distinguished gentleman who invented the telephone, the metal detector, and the hydrofoil. It explains why his former Canadian residence is a National Historic Site, and why it is located in Baddeck, Cape Breton. The question is: Why did Cape Breton beat out the Rockies, Andes, Highlands, and Alps? Why do international travel magazines bestow titles on Cape Breton including "The Most Scenic Island in the World" (*Condé Nast*), "The Number One Island to Visit in Continental North America" (*Travel+Leisure*), and "One of the World's Greatest Destinations" (*National*

Geographic)? If Cape Breton casts a spell on its visitors, what lies behind its McAbracadabra?

Aye, the Scottish influence is unmistakable. Upwards of fifty thousand Highlanders found their way to Cape Breton in the early nineteenth century, bringing their Gaelic language and culture with them. Centuries later, discovering Scotland in Canada charms the kilt off most visitors, unaccustomed to the distinct Cape Breton accent they encounter in small communities dotting the island. You will also discover some wonderfully preserved Acadian communities — Belle Côte, Terre Noire, Cap Le Moine, Grand Étang, Chéticamp — benefiting from their isolation, adapted to the distinct environmental culture of the Maritimes.

I crossed the island's causeway on the very day a Cape Breton musical legend, Buddy MacMaster, passed away. Fiddlers would be gathering from around the world, and it is fiddle music I heard just about it everywhere, starting at the Celtic Music Interpretive Centre in Judique. Here I would also experience my first *ceilidh* (pronounced kay-lee), a traditional gathering of song and dance. My own fiddle efforts in the museum sounded not unlike a cat sliding down a three-storey chalkboard, claws extended. And let's not get into my Highland dancing efforts.

Cape Breton Island has several immaculate driving routes. Motorbikes, cars, bicycles, and RVs descend in their thousands each summer to explore the meandering, hilly coastal roads, the cyclists receiving a certain amount of pity and respect when you pass them. There are world-renowned golf resorts, sailing on the sparkling inland sea of Bras d'Or, and worthy attractions like the Alexander Graham Bell Museum, Glace Bay's Coal Miner Museum, and the Fortress of Louisbourg [see page 64]. Kayaking up the North River on a sunny day was entirely memorable, complete with a shower in a local waterfall and a blues-jam session with owner/musician Antonio Spinazzola. Islanders have fantastic stories to tell, and even better musical skills for the soundtrack.

The Cabot Trail is an approximately three-hundred-kilometre loop at the northern tip of Cape Breton, running through eight com-

The End of Cabot's Trail

Italian explorer Giovanni Caboto, a.k.a. Jean Cabot, a.k.a. Juan Cabot, a.k.a. John Cabot, a.k.a. Zuan Chabatto, was commissioned by Henry VII of England to find a faster sailing route to Asia. In doing so, he became the first European since the Vikings to land on mainland North America, in what Canadian and U.K. historians agree was Cape Bonavista, Newfoundland. Rather skittishly, Cabot did not explore much farther than the rich offshore cod stocks. After a hero's welcome back in England, he mustered up some ships for a return voyage and was promptly never heard from again. Historians question whether he was lost at sea, settled in North America or returned to obscurity in England. ➤

munities (Scottish, Irish, and Acadian), across the Margaree River, and the island's crown jewel, the 948-square-kilometre Cape Breton Highlands National Park. Open year-round, the Cabot Trail could put together its own Top 10 list of how many Top 10 lists it has been placed on. It is a destination worthy of the acclaim. Summers are gorgeous, while foliage explodes each fall for the Celtic Colours International Festival. Shaped by the Gulf of St. Lawrence on the west and the Atlantic on the east, the national park consists of temperate and boreal forest containing bird species you won't find anywhere else in the country.

Communities come alive for the occasion. The Acadian fishing village of Chéticamp welcomes tourists with fiddle music and traditional hooked rugs, while Ingonish, at the east entrance to the national park, touts one of Canada's most highly rated golf courses, the Stanley Thompson–designed eighteen-hole Highlands Links Golf Course.

But it's the mountains on the elevated plateau that left the biggest impression, rolling into the sea, a million-dollar view waiting around every corner. Some of the park's two-dozen hikes, the most popular being the Panorama, take you right to the cliff edge of the headlands. In Pleasant Bay, I hopped onboard Captain Mark's Whale Cruise, and even if forty pilot whales hadn't surrounded our boat and sung their riddles for our underwater cameras, the views of the Highlands rolling into the Atlantic would have been worth it.

Throughout the island, keep your eyes peeled for all-age community ceilidhs, delicious lobster suppers, and flowing pints of the

local craft ale, Big Spruce. You'll quickly notice this is a place where locals smile with their mouths, eyes, and hearts.

Yes, one can spend a week or a lifetime enjoying Cape Breton, taking in its sights, meeting its people, and experiencing its history. A week or a lifetime to agree with the opinions of nineteenth-century inventors, round-ups in twenty-first century travel magazines, and writers of national bucket lists.

START HERE: canadianbucketlist.com/capebreton

Dram Good Whisky

With Cape Breton's rich Scottish heritage, consider popping into North America's first single malt whisky distillery, Glenora. Located on Highway 19, take a distillery tour before tasting the impact of Cape Breton ambiance on aging oak casks. There's a wonderful inn and restaurant on-site, too. ➤

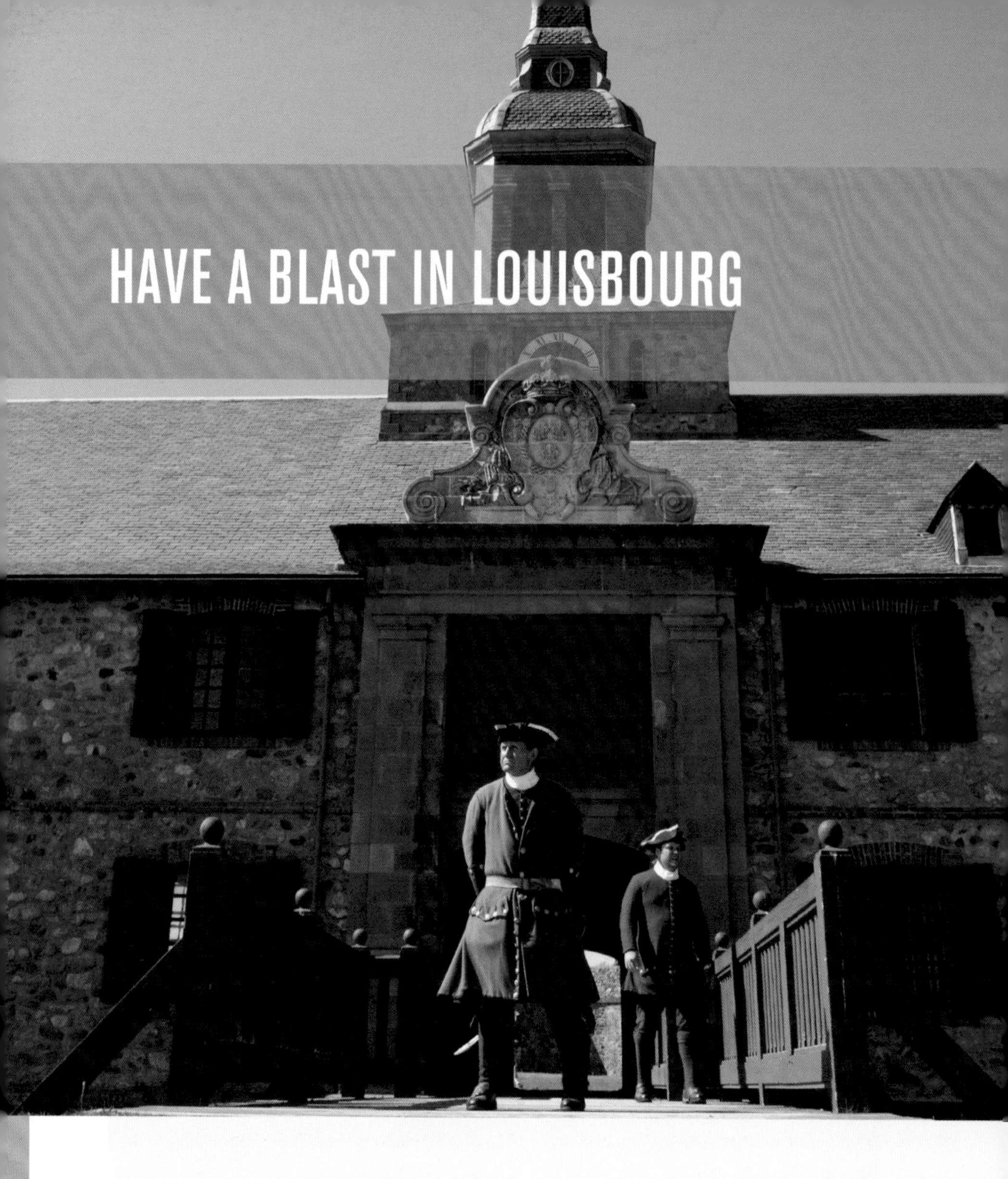

HAVE A BLAST IN LOUISBOURG

You won't understand just how big and ambitious Parks Canada's Louisbourg Fortress is until you see it. You'll quickly realize why this National Historic Site is the largest historical reconstruction project in North America. Completely rebuilt based on meticulous records kept by the French government, the fortress takes you back to the year 1744, when French soldiers protected a lucrative cod outpost. Levelled by the British during the Seven Years' War, Louisbourg

rotted on the coast for two hundred years until the federal government saw it as an opportunity for unemployed coal miners in the 1960s — and, of course, to reclaim an important part of Canadian history. Much like the Halifax Citadel, re-enactors add colour to this living museum, and help visitors make traditional cookies on the fire, tend the flock, or light the two twelve o'clock cannons. Provided with formal eighteenth-century French army uniforms, it's worth paying a little extra for the half-hour Cannoneer in Training program. Space is limited, so call to book ahead. Regardless of your level of affection for French colonial artillery science, our bucket list has plenty of room for the Louisbourg boom.

START HERE: canadianbucketlist.com/louisbourg

PRINCE EDWARD ISLAND

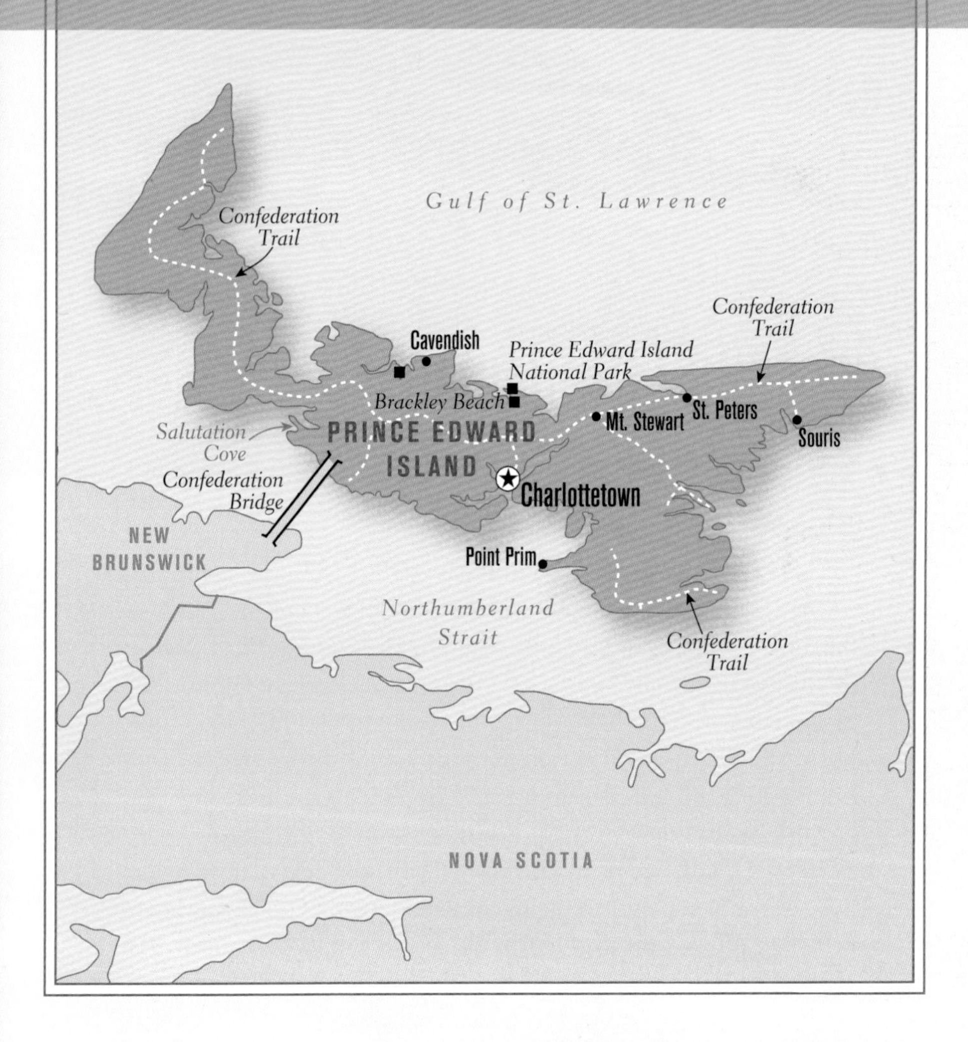

CYCLE ACROSS THE GENTLE ISLAND

There's a lot to be said for multi-day cycling trips. Awakening our five senses, we can smell our surroundings, taste the wind, see the trails cut across rolling hills, listen to birdsong, and feel wonderful that we're burning calories in the process. Yet, since I'm nowhere in the kind of shape I should be, the thought of a long bike trip is physically daunting. How many times have I driven past a cyclist huffing up a big hill and thought: "I wouldn't want to be *that* poor bastard!" I do enjoy cycling, downhill usually, joyrides mostly. A week on a saddle seems like a callused and sore arse waiting to happen, but undeniably it remains an experience worth doing before pedalling off into the sky. If only there was somewhere mostly flat, somewhere with scenic beauty, friendly locals, and delicious cuisine.

Somewhere that will allow me to stay in charming B&Bs and inns and have my bags shuttled ahead for me? Somewhere like Prince Edward Island.

Canada's smallest province appears to have been designed for amateur cyclists like me (and for you hardcore folks, as well). Besides its abundant bike lanes, P.E.I. is blessed with a mostly flat trail that snakes from the west coast to the east, a 470-kilometre tip-to-tip marvel known as the Confederation Trail. Arteries branch to coastal communities, linking to paved bike lanes that skirt some of the most magnificent scenery in the country. Some of you might prefer to plan every step of the way yourself. I contacted outdoor specialists Great Canadian Trails, who make it as easy as coasting down a hill. Together with a highly knowledgeable and immensely likeable islander named George Larter, they offer the ultimate P.E.I. cycling trip. All we have to do is show up. George picks us up from the airport, shuttling us over to the Outer Limit Bike Shop to pick up our rental bikes. If, like me, you have no idea what a pannier is, don't fret. These bike bags are straddled onto comfortable upright hybrid bikes, which in turn are strapped onto George's van to take us to our first stop. Now all we have to do is pedal. George will ensure our luggage is waiting at our next inn, always close to a cold Gahan wheat ale and that famous P.E.I. seafood. Really, it's as simple as riding a bike.

We start in the town of Borden-Carleton, in sight of the Confederation Bridge (see page 84). Replacing a dug-up rail track, the well-maintained Confederation Trail is a car-width wide gravel strip cutting through dense forests, rural villages, and fertile farmland. It's a hot summer day, and our handy itinerary is blessedly flexible. Since this is only Day One, we let enthusiasts tackle the extra twenty-four kilometres to Kensington, and instead leave the trail after eighteen kilometres for the lightly trafficked shouldered highway that leads to Stanley Bridge. Bright sunshine reflects the countryside off our sunglasses. We see manicured lawns bigger than football fields, sprawling fields of potatoes, lush meadows, and purple lupines cradling immaculate wooden houses. All the peacefulness and beauty of the gentle island floods our five senses. Arriving at the Stanley Bridge Resort, bags waiting for us in large air-conditioned rooms, we're physically knackered, but not enough to deny ourselves the reward of a dozen fresh oysters at the adjacent Carr's Oyster Bar. Day One may have been physical, but it was also a slow seduction into the island's pace. Day Two will clobber us over the head, grab us by the hair, and carry us back to the cave.

It's called the Gulf Shore Parkway, and it is, without doubt, one of the world's most beautiful bike rides. From Cavendish (see page 90), we follow a paved bike path onto the beach, and ride east into Prince Edward Island National Park. Tracing the shoreline, the fifty-kilometre parkway takes us to tall sand dunes, windswept beaches, viewing decks, and P.E.I.'s striking red coastline. With postcard-worthy views around every bend, and having had more than enough time to explore them, we arrive in North Rustico elated. That Parkway is truly something special. Waiting for us at Fisherman's Wharf is a lobster supper, a wooden boardwalk to bike off the all-you-can-eat dessert tray, and a smiling George, ready to shuttle us along to Brackley Bay. We could ride there ourselves, but there's no shoulder on the highway and too many hills. Let's save our time and energy for the good stuff!

After a relaxing overnight cabin stay at Shaw's (the oldest business on the island), we continue the following morning on the paved parkway, hop onto some quiet local roads, and re-join the Confederation Trail en route to Mount Stewart. Awaiting us is offbeat accommodation above the homely, rustic Trailside Café. Each room here has a vintage record player, and a choice selection of vinyl selected by owners Pat and Meghann Deighan, who also happen to own Charlottetown's hippest record store.

"Everyone in P.E.I. tells a good story and plays an instrument," a friend once told me. We hear great stories and incredible music at the café downstairs, which features local and touring musicians each summer weekend. The place is jammed and the staff as welcoming as good friends — which by the end of the night, they are.

Just steps from our antique bed frame, the bike path continues east to St. Peters, crossing pink-painted wooden bridges, peat bogs, bubbling streams, and hardwood forests. The thirteen kilometres from Morrell to St. Peters is considered among the most scenic sections of the entire Confederation Trail. Oyster and mussel beds line the inlets. With our legs getting stronger, the kilometres disappear behind us with increasing quickness. That night, we will toast the moon as it lights the gazebo beneath the Inn at St. Peters. Wine will flow. All of us "from-aways" — whether we're travelling by car, motorbike, or bicycle — recognize that a golden P.E.I. summer is worthy of celebration.

The next day it's all trail from St. Peters to the coastal town of Souris: our final stop. A week ago, I'd never have imagined myself biking forty kilometres in a single morning; much less that I'd have the legs to continue if I wanted (the itinerary includes an optional forty-seven-kilometre circle route to Basin Head Provincial Park).

Adjacent to the historic McLean House Inn in Souris is a local eatery called the Bluefin. We reward ourselves with their surf and turf — an eight-ounce rib-eye steak and a pound and a half of lobster — all for less than thirty dollars.

It has been an unforgettable week relishing the beauty of Prince Edward Island — keeping healthy, making friends, and eating "like a King in France," as the Germans would say. Listening to the wind blowing in from the Gulf of St Lawrence, how could we not fall asleep with a smile on our faces? This is a one-of-a-kind trip for experienced cyclists — and for the rest of us, too.

START HERE: canadianbucketlist.com/bikeP.E.I.

HAUL A LOBSTER TRAP

Lobsters intimidate me. For starters, they look like miniature spider-dragon aliens, capable of slicing your neck off with one swipe of their giant claw, or latching onto your face to impregnate you with acid-dripping offspring. Just look at their undersides: surely that was the inspiration for the monsters in the *Alien* movies. Spiky legs, sharp edges, and two beady eyes thinking, "If I were your size and you were mine ..." Growing up inland, I never had lobster on the menu, and while I appreciate it is a delicacy for many, so are crickets in Thailand, worms in Venezuela, and deep-fried guinea pig in Ecuador. So it is with some trepidation that I step onto Perry Gotell's boat at 4:00 a.m., ready to experience the real working life of an East Coast lobster fisherman.

It's hard work, and the season is short. Six days a week for two solid months, Perry and his first mate, Jerry Mackenzie, motor out into the bay to haul in their three hundred wooden traps and deliver a lucrative load for distributors back at the dock. Blessed with a calm, clear morning, I slip on my waterproofs and get to work before we even leave the dock. A huge blue tub of mackerel must be cut up for each lobster trap. Before the sun breaches the horizon, my rubber gloves are covered in grungy, smelly fish guts. Perry is a third-generation lobster fisherman, and his traps sit at the bottom of the same waters his family have been fishing for decades.

With Perry steering the boat and keying in the GPS coordinates of the traps, Jerry takes a long pole to hook each trap's buoy, attach it to a mechanical crane, and begin hauling heavy wooden crates onto the side of the boat. With dozens of lobster-fishing boats around us, the industry is heavily regulated to ensure there is no overfishing. Licences cost well into the six figures, and while a good day out can yield thousands of dollars, it's hard, relentless work with plenty of costs to go with it. Perry spends about $1,200 a week just for his bait.

But disembowelled flounder and mackerel are the least of my worries. The traps are literally crawling with huge crabs and panicky large lobsters. Both have sharp claws, protected by strong shells.

"Go ahead," says Perry. "Stick your hand in and start sorting 'em."

Lobsters with black eggs are immediately tossed back into the sea to produce new yields. Only the largest crabs are collected, to be weighed and sold; the rest also find themselves sinking back to the bottom of the Atlantic Ocean. The lobsters themselves are put in a sorting bin, from which Jerry measures their size and determines whether they are classed as premium market or standard "canned." Market lobsters have their claws banded with small blue elastics to

prevent them from damaging one another. New bait is set by placing chunks of mackerel on a spike or in a vise inside each trap.

Perry locates a preferable spot and the traps are dumped overboard for another day to do their job. We repeat the above for eight hours, ticking off each of the fifty buoys and mentally counting down each of the three hundred traps. Perry's ideal is to catch old, huge, and heavy lobsters, which he calls "bone crushers" for the size of their claws. At the start of the season, a typical day might net 550 kilograms of lobster, but today, toward the end, he'll be lucky to get 135 kilograms. Since fishermen are paid by weight, I can't imagine what it must be like to work four times harder than this.

Meanwhile, I'm still getting over the fear that a crab might sever an artery, or a lobster snip off a finger. "They're smaller than me and their brains are the size of a pinhead. Outthink, Outsmart, Out . . . oh, to hell with it, come here, you ugly crustacean!" Within a few hours I'm sweeping traps clear in seconds. The sunrise is spectacular, and being able to see the red cliffs of the island helps with my sea legs, along with the added distraction of listening to Perry and Jerry's salty dog stories. Each trap presents its own challenge, its own hope of a monster haul or a better one tomorrow.

I'd spent the morning out in the elements, working with nature's bounty, conquering my fears and learning about a fascinating industry. Hard work, yes, but what an experience. "One guy, he told us fishin' lobster was on his bucket list," says Jerry, rinsing the boat. Turns out that guy wasn't alone.

Catching lobster might be hard work, but eating them isn't. Fisherman's Wharf in North Rustico has tanks for 26,000 pounds of lobster, served pounds at a time with an all-you-can-eat salad bar. Charlottetown's Water Prince Corner Shop and Lobster Pound is another good bet. Crack the claw, extract the meat, chew the tail, suck the legs, and, if you're into the delicacy of organs, savour the tomalley.

START HERE: canadianbucketlist.com/lobster

TONG AND SHUCK OYSTERS

I had tasted Prince Edward Island long before I ever stepped foot in the province. After all, P.E.I. mussels, oysters, and lobsters are much-prized items on restaurant menus across North America. I looked forward to tucking into this seafood bonanza as soon as I arrived, especially oysters — that delectable bivalve long associated with decadent pleasure. Some people might argue there's nothing delicious about consuming a live, raw animal with the texture of a nasal infection. Some people need to get into the spirit of things. To help, experience the life of an oyster farmer in the field — or, more accurately, the water — through a "Tong & Shuck" activity offered by Salutation Cove's Rocky Bay Oysters.

Co-owner Erskine Lewis takes me out on a boat into the shallow waters of the cove, where oysters grow naturally in abundance. After demonstrating the art of tonging oysters from the sandy depths, Erskine hands me the wooden rake-like tool with stainless steel teeth. I carefully scrape the bottom, jostling the tong to loosen up the oysters and hopefully bring in a decent haul. It takes a few tries before I get the hang of it, but my hauls are still a fraction of Erskine's.

How to Shuck an Oyster

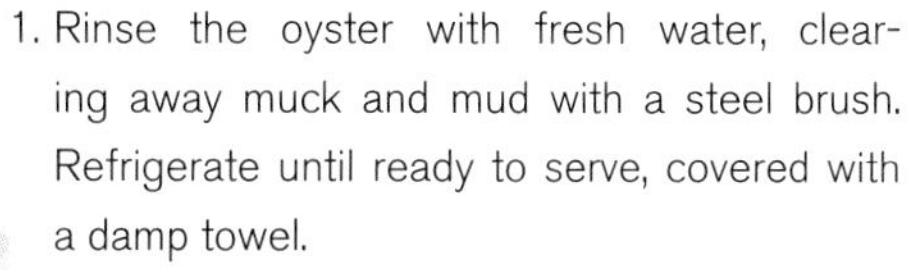

1. Rinse the oyster with fresh water, clearing away muck and mud with a steel brush. Refrigerate until ready to serve, covered with a damp towel.

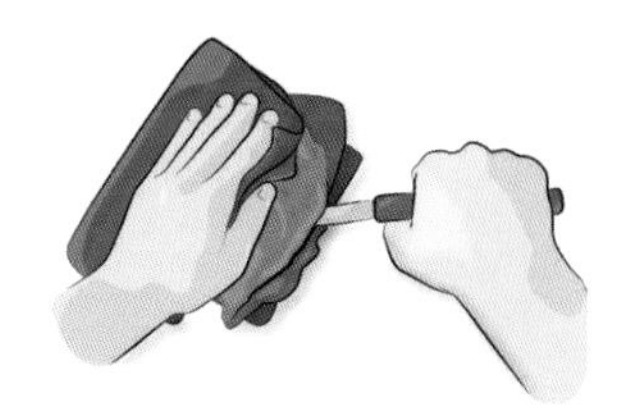

2. Use a dishtowel or glove to protect yourself as you hold the oyster down on a flat surface, the pointed hinge facing you. Insert the oyster knife into the hinge, pushing it toward the bottom of the cup and giving it a slight wiggle. Twist the knife to pop the hinge.

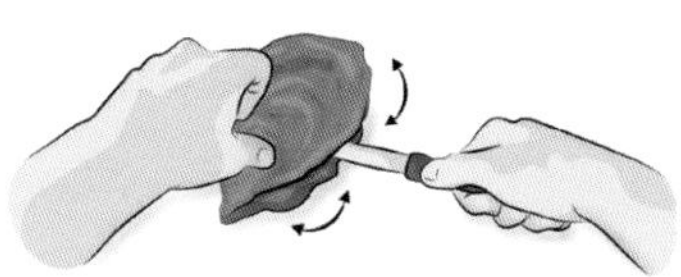

3. To cut the muscles holding the shell together, slide the knife across the top of the shell. Separate the shell, clear away any mess, and slide the knife under the oyster flesh to detach it from the bottom shell. ➤

We measure the size of each oyster against a simple measuring unit, returning the ones that don't make the cut. Erskine explains that the difference between choice, restaurant-grade oysters and standard, industrial oysters is simply the shape of the shell. The more round, the more sought-after, and often the less actual oyster to slurp back. Erskine rummages through my haul, selects a choice shell, shucks it right there and hands it to me. No lemon juice, no Tabasco. P.E.I. oysters are best enjoyed raw, fresh, and on their own. For this is no ordinary oyster: this is the very taste of Salutation Cove, nature condensed into a food group.

In just a couple of hours, I develop a deep respect for oysters, and the amount of work it takes to grow, harvest, and distribute them. The price of an oyster in a P.E.I. restaurant: $2.50. Being able to appreciate them: priceless.

It was time to put the oysters into their more familiar context, and so I enlisted the help of a true oyster aficionado. John Bil is a three-time Canadian Oyster Shucking Champion, a man who believes

the ocean does all the work, while chefs just add the heat. After teaching me how to shuck an oyster and demonstrating his own renowned skill (including shucking blindfolded, behind his back), John educates me on the subtleties of oyster appreciation. And sure enough, I begin to taste the coves from which they were harvested, feeling the waves in my mouth.

At Carr's Oyster Bar, an island institution located over the bridge in scenic Stanley Bridge, I order a dozen world-renowned Malpeque oysters — fresh from the nearby beds. John Bil started his career shucking oysters at Carr's. Each bivalve seems to tell a story of the waters, land, and people of the island. Or maybe I was drunk on the wheat-honey ale. Either way, these oysters represent bivalves at their finest, and in a fine environment, too.

Why are P.E.I. oysters so revered? "Oysters are like grapes. A Sauvignon Blanc from Ontario is simply not the same as a Sauvignon Blanc from California," explains John. From which I conclude that an oyster tonged in P.E.I.'s coves is unlike an oyster from anywhere else, and its taste belongs on our bucket list.

START HERE: canadianbucketlist.com/oysters

PLAY A ROUND OF GOLF

There are several things I look forward to doing in the autumn years of my life. I look forward to watching all these TV shows people keep talking about, so I can finally visit Westeros, and understand why the phrase "winter is coming" is significant. I look forward to a long career in skydiving, weeks spent playing video games, hip replacements, and, most of all, golf. Not all at the same time, mind you, although that would be interesting.

You see, golf demands the supreme patience, time, skill and budget reserves I don't yet possess. For those who argue the folly of whacking a little ball a long way to get it into a little cup, I say, "Four!" Yes, I spelled that correctly.

One: Golf gets you outside, in the fresh air, usually in beautiful surroundings.
Two: Golf gets you socially active, because really, it's not all that important whether you score a birdie or an eagle or any other form of bird life.
Three: Golf is a personal challenge, a combination of mental and physical skill that is easy to learn and impossible to master. Just ask Tiger Woods's ex-wife.
Four: Golf is punctuated by ice-cold beverages and ends in a clubhouse with more libations, nachos, and chicken wings.

Prince Edward Island may be Canada's smallest, least-populated province, but the facts speak for themselves: At the time of writing, it claims ten out of the Top 100 Golf Courses as rated by *Globe and Mail* readers, and 5 percent of the Top 350 Courses in North America. The island is branded as Canada's Number One Golf Destination, and received an award from the International Association of Golf Travel Operators as the Undiscovered Golf Destination of the Year. The island's thirty-three courses (at the time of writing) are renowned for their natural beauty, variety, design, and the fact that they're mostly a half-hour drive from Charlottetown.

Take the Brudenell River Golf Club, one of the island's most popular courses, dotted with lakes, ponds and gardens. Here I have the opportunity to learn a few tricks from LPGA pro and resident island golf expert Anne Chouinard. Considering my experience is mostly limited to hacking the carpet off minigolf courses, Anne is impressed by my enthusiasm. She moved here from Quebec for the fantastic island lifestyle along with the world-class courses, and she recommends anyone with a love of the game do so as well.

We proceed to play a round, the course buttressing against a gorgeous coastline, surrounded by the tranquility of Brudenell Provincial

Feed Giant Bluefin Tuna

Tuna might look benign and flaky in your sandwich, but they are impressive ocean predators. Gathering in large numbers out of North Lake, anglers battle giant bluefins on catch-and-release charters. The rest of us can enjoy feeding herring to the tuna, which move alarmingly fast for five-hundred-kilogram fish. ➤

Park. At par-three, I somehow manage to skip my golf ball twice over a water hazard and into the rough. Anne tells me Phil Mickelson did that once on purpose, which I take as a compliment. On the sixth hole, I'm pretty sure I scored a puffin, penguin, and pigeon, which is definitely quite the feat. This demands further celebration back at the clubhouse, with nachos and cold beer. Despite Anne's best efforts, I have a lot to learn if I want to master this game. Before I die, there's no place I'd rather master it than on Prince Edward Island.

START HERE: canadianbucketlist.com/golf

CROSS CONFEDERATION BRIDGE

At the birth pang of Canada, when the founding provinces gathered for the Charlottetown Conference, tiny Prince Edward Island was only accessible by ferry. It may have been Canada through and through, but it wasn't physically connected to Canada, and winter ferry crossings could be notoriously dicey. A century later, a debate raged about the merits of building a massive bridge to connect the island to the New Brunswick mainland. The Islanders for a Better Tomorrow argued for the economic benefits of building such a bridge, in terms of both trade and tourism. Friends of the Island felt their lifestyles were under threat and said that not enough research had been done (or indeed could ever be done) to justify the expense. They even tried a legal blockade, but lost when a judge ruled the environmental assessment was adequate. Finally, it came down to a

vote in which Islanders were asked if they were in favour of replacing the ferries with an unspecified alternative. In January 1988, a resounding 59.4 percent voted yes to the fixed link. Four years and one billion dollars later, the 12.9-kilometre Confederation Bridge opened for traffic.

Many years later, I found myself in a car about to make this remarkable crossing. It was summer, so the fact that this is the world's longest bridge over ice-covered water didn't impress me. Nor did the pricey round-trip toll, although if there's one bridge that doesn't give you much of an option, this is it (ferry service was discontinued when the bridge opened). Once I had passed the toll on the East Bridge Approach, the fact that I was on an engineering marvel that once employed over five thousand people and boosted the province's

GDP during construction by 5 percent was kind of lost on me as well. What impressed me deeply was my car cruising at eighty kilometres per hour, surrounded on either side by the cold, dark waters of the Atlantic. The architects had thoughtfully curved the bridge to ensure distracted drivers like myself would pay attention to the road, and not launch off the bridge to add motor vehicles to the marine life below. The highest curve — known as the Navigation Span — is sixty metres above seawater, which is ample height for cruise ships and tankers to pass underneath, between piers spaced 250 metres apart. For those more nervous than myself, rest easy: there are twenty-two surveillance cameras, seven thousand drain ports, emergency alarms, strict speed limits, and a surface designed to minimize water spray. The bridge was built to last one hundred years, by which time we should be making the crossing in flying cars anyway.

Confederation Bridge is more than just a homegrown mega-industrial project, full of impressive numbers and statistics that hopefully kept you entertained. It's an umbilical cord of national pride, a symbol of democracy, and a fast, efficient way to get to a truly lovely destination.

START HERE: canadianbucketlist.com/confederation

HARVEST SEA PLANTS

Writing in a pirate voice is not the same as speaking in a pirate voice, but I'm going to give it a shot anyway: "Yargh! The sea holds a rich bounty of deliciousness, yargh!"

I was hoping the wonderfully named Gilbert and Goldie Gillis would also speak in pirate, since they comb the nearby beaches for buried treasure, albeit treasure of a different sort. They greet me at their B&B, which, like many houses in P.E.I., is surrounded by lawns so immaculate one could relocate the courts of Wimbledon here. The couple is so sweet and earnest I want them to adopt me. Together they have lived here much of their lives, married in the shadow of the same Point Prim lighthouse that Gilbert's grandfather once kept, the oldest lighthouse in the province.

Get to the treasure, yargh!

Quick Guide to Edible Sea Plants

Dulse: Soft and chewy, distinctive taste and colour, requires no soaking or cooking, great in soups and sandwiches.

Irish moss: Bushy red plant, traditionally boiled to release carrageenan, a natural gelling agent used as a thickener in food and cosmetics.

Sea lettuce: Leafy, dark green, with distinctive flavour, good raw but can be bitter when cooked. Used in soups and salads. High in protein, iron, and fibre.

Kelp: Grouped in the same family as algae, typically used in Japanese or Chinese cooking to flavour stews and soups, or served as a pickled garnish. ➤

The Gillises have been harvesting seaweed and crafting seaweed dishes for generations, an art and hobby they now share through a program called Seaweed Secrets.

"We want to introduce people to the medicinal and nutritional value of all living sea plants," explains Gilbert, and proceeds to do so. We hop in his pickup truck and head over to beautiful Point Prim, the calm sea sparkling in the sun. It's low tide, so we scamper onto some rocks to see what's stacked on the ocean shelves. Irish moss, dulse, kelp, sea lettuce — it looks like rotten veggies, the stuff you avoid when swimming, or the gunk that might get tangled in your outboard motor. Gilbert begs to differ.

"Look at this Irish moss. It has carrageenan, which is used like gelatin," he says, picking it off a rock. The moss is rich in nutrients and can be used in all sorts of dishes. Gilbert gets excited when he spots a plant called devil's shoelace. When it dries out, it can be added to salad to add a taste not unlike crispy bacon. Then there's gracilaria, a sea plant that grows on the shells of oysters and mussels. Goldie is famous for her Wild Island Teriyaki Pickled Seaweed made from the stuff.

Back at the B&B, the Gillises have assembled an edible Sea Plant Museum in their garden barn with the aid of a botanist. I tuck into a bag of dried sea lettuce, an alga that is high in protein, fibre, vitamins, and minerals. It tastes like mouldy salt. Although sea lettuce is widely

eaten around the world, traditional lettuce can feel safe for now; but then again, typical lettuce might not give you that Gillis gleam. Goldie looks radiant, her skin smooth and her hair full of body, all attributed to homemade cosmetics made of, what else, sea plants.

In the kitchen, Goldie's got some seaweed vegetable soup on the stove. None of the plants really look edible until they reach her kitchen. She gives some moss a thorough rinse and puts it in a blender. It's then whisked with sugar and vanilla, poured into a base of breadcrumbs and baked. Topped with fresh cream and home-grown rhubarb confit, the result is a custard-like tart that's as good as any I've ever tasted. Not bad for the stuff I was walking on just a couple of hours ago on the beach. We toast the sunset with a sea-plant buffet (damn, those are some fine pickles) and the fact that every day edible treasures are being washed up on the beach. Yargh to that!

START HERE: canadianbucketlist.com/seaplants

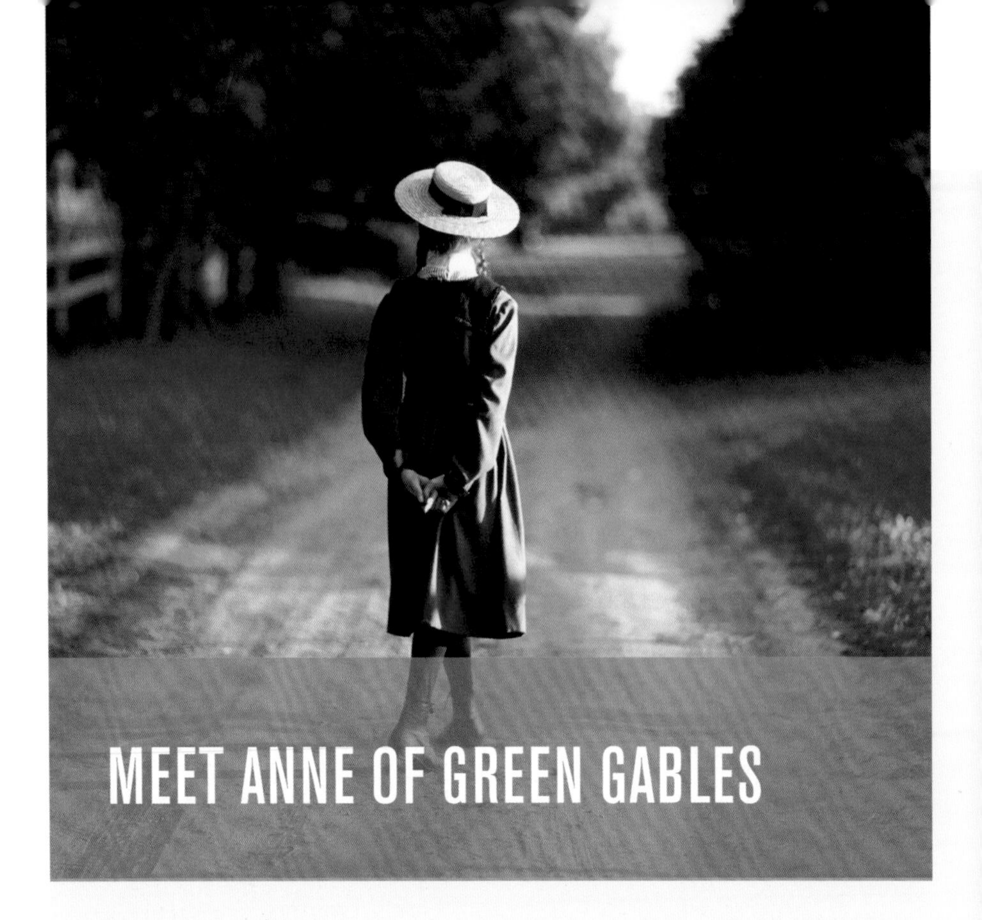

MEET ANNE OF GREEN GABLES

Long, long, long before *Harry Potter* and *Twilight*, another epic children's book series crossed into the mainstream to become an international publishing phenomenon. It followed the life and misadventures of a red-headed, freckled orphan with sparkling green eyes. Set among the rolling green fields and small-town shenanigans of Prince Edward Island, Lucy Maud Montgomery's *Anne of Green Gables*, and the eight sequels that followed, immersed readers in the daily lives of early-twentieth-century P.E.I. citizens. Written over a period of nearly fifteen years, the books follow Anne's evolution from scrappy kid to educated young lady to poised and upright citizen, from age eleven to her late fifties. Anne resonated around the world, with over 50 million books sold, numerous accolades for her author, and the distinction of being both a Canadian and a Japanese cultural icon. Montgomery's genius lay not only in the richness of her characters but also in her descriptions of the world in which they

Anne of Japan

Canada's best-known fictional character still resonates around the world, which is why, growing up in South Africa, I had a prepubescent crush on Megan Follows. But the adventures of the feisty orphan really hit a nerve in Japan, where she is known as *Akage no An*, literally "Anne of the Red Hair." Anne's independence strongly appealed to Japanese girls confined by society, and Prince Edward Island's natural setting appealed to their sense of fantasy. Ever since the books were first translated in the early 1950s, Anne has become a Japanese superstar. You can buy her products, watch her on TV, and visit a Green Gables theme park in Ashibetsu City, Hokkaido. ➤

operated. Prince Edward Island's allure as a destination is assured with anyone who reads *Anne of Green Gables*, including school kids in Japan who continue to do so. I, too, was required to visit the fields of Cavendish and Avonlea as a student in South Africa. No surprise, then, that thousands of Canadian and international visitors beeline to the inspiration behind the books, along with a range of attractions honouring the Maritimes' most famous literary hero.

Green Gables Heritage Place is just part of Lucy Maud Montgomery's Cavendish National Historic Site. Visitors can explore the original farmhouse, which belonged to cousins of Montgomery's grandfather, along with the Haunted Woods and Lovers Lane that inspired places of the same names in the books. Green Gables

continues to receive around 350,000 visitors a year. In the capital, July to September sees the annual production of *Anne of Green Gables — The Musical* at the Charlottetown Festival. Adapted from the book, the musical has been running for five decades and is performed at the Confederation Centre of the Arts. A half-hour's drive away you'll find Avonlea: Village of Anne of Green Gables, a historical village that re-creates the life and times of Prince Edward Island in the early 1900s. Character actors and horses and buggies roam about the village, with visitors popping into musical kitchen parties, plays from the books, and Anne-branded chocolate factories and ice-cream parlours. If you get thirsty, grab a bottle of official Anne-branded raspberry cordial, her much-loved bright red drink.

Yes, enterprising Anne, in the form of the Anne of Green Gables Licensing Authority Inc., is not one to let a merchandising opportunity pass her by. Neither would P.E.I.'s provincial government, which owns half of the corporation, with the other half owned by

Montgomery's descendants. Hence the trove of Anne-branded merchandise available at the Anne of Green Gables Store, eagerly snapped up by Japanese tourists. The Japanese love *Anne* as much as *Alice in Wonderland*, which is why you'll probably see Japanese tourists hanging about the site of Lucy Maud Montgomery's Cavendish home, some of them in full costume.

If you don't know *Anne of Green Gables*, or have no interest in the antics of conservative, religious Maritime society, you're free to swap this item for something like, say, a visit to the sweeping Greenwich Dunes in Prince Edward Island National Park. This rare coastal dune system and its adjacent wetlands have beautiful walking trails and a long white wooden boardwalk that glows with life at sunset. But when it comes to realizing a fantasy world, kudos to P.E.I.'s Anne attractions for living up to our imaginations.

START HERE: canadianbucketlist.com/gables

NEWFOUNDLAND AND LABRADOR

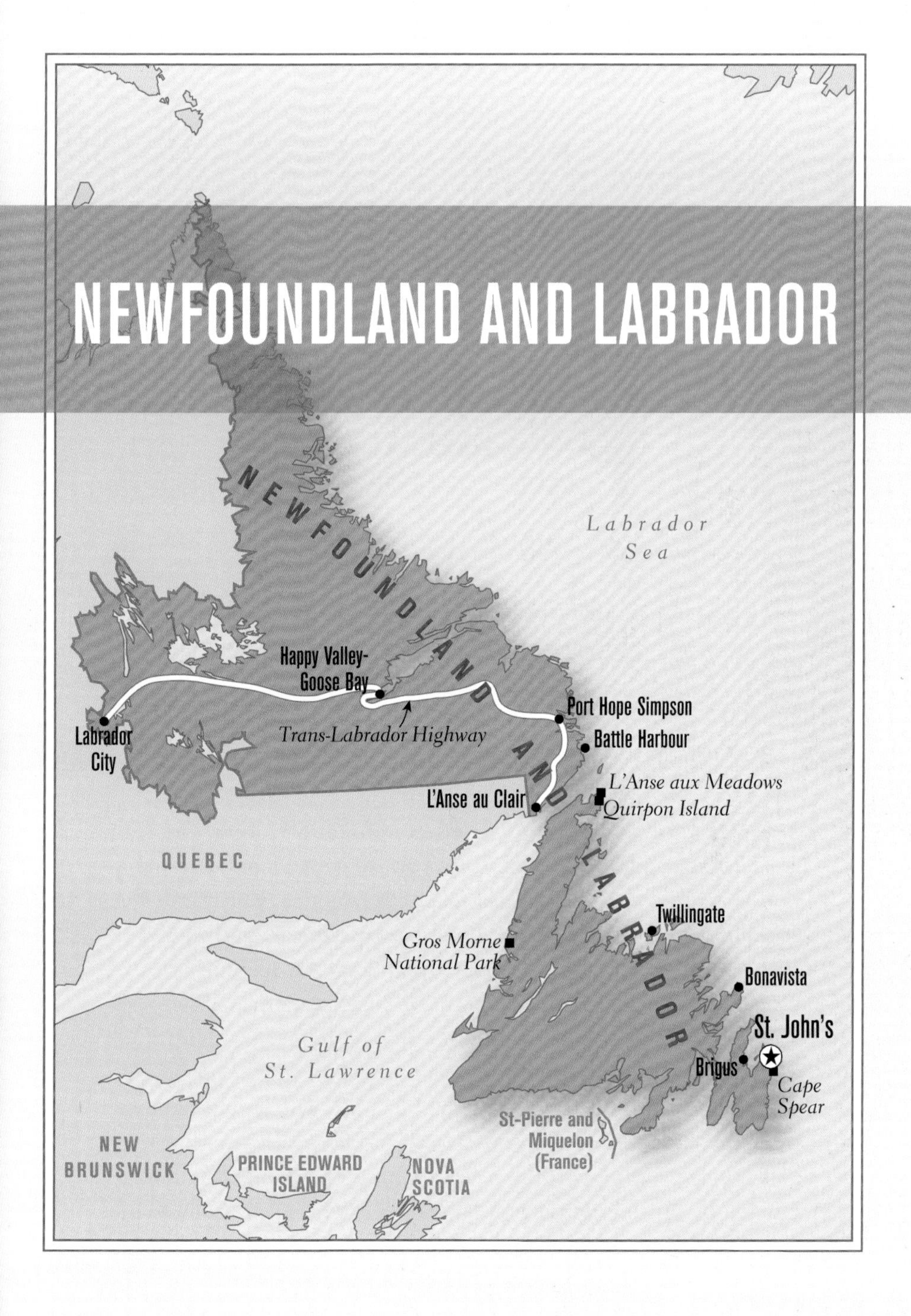

WATCH THE SUN RISE ON A CONTINENT

Having arrived late the previous evening in St. John's, and with just four pitiful hours of sleep, I awake with a fool's determination to witness the first sunrise in North America. Just twenty-five minutes' drive away from my hotel is Cape Spear, the most easterly point in Canada and, notwithstanding the technicalities of Greenland, the most easterly point of North America. When you have but one morning in St. John's, you have to make it count.

Sunrises are more glorious than sunsets, because you have to work much harder to witness them. No "relax with a glass of wine" moments here, but just as sunsets seal the day, early morning egg-yolk sunrises bring with them the promise of unlimited potential. Excited by this thought, I pull back the curtains at my hotel to see fog so thick you could float a sumo wrestler on it. St. John's is famous

Wind, Rain, and Fog

Don't be too upset if your sunset is also draped in fog. With 121 foggy days a year, St. John's is Canada's foggiest city, not to mention the windiest. Take comfort that the wind blows away the fog (along with the occasional household pet). ➤

for this atmospheric fog, which is great if your life is a film noir mystery but rather inconvenient for sunrise hunters.

Fortified with strong coffee and hope, I hop in the car and direct the GPS toward Cape Spear. The roads at this time of day are desolate. Lonely metal clangs on the big fishing ships along Marine Drive. I follow directions to Water Street and turn left onto Blackhead Road as the car's headlights reflect back at me in the fog. There's a dirty light in the air, as if the sun is feeling ill and doesn't want to get out of bed. The car passes wooden houses, dispersed farther and farther apart, and just as I begin to relax into the ambience of driving inside a cloud, I catch a movement in the trees up ahead. A large moose jumps out in front of me, causing me to brake hard and wake up everyone within miles with a panicked thumping on my horn. Seriously, Moose, you've got the whole province to roam about in, why throw the tourist a surprise party at dawn?

I'd been warned about moose on the roads in Newfoundland, which appear to toy with cars on purpose, like spiteful teenagers annoying authority. The moose vanishes into the brush, leaving me a shot of early morning adrenalin more powerful than any espresso. Minutes later I arrive at the Cape Spear National Historic Site, the parking lot deserted. Clearly, I'm the only person optimistic enough

to believe in a foggy sunrise. The wind is howling, the air is wet, I'm cursing luck, weather, and moose, when I stop dead in my tracks. The full power of the North Atlantic, crashing into the rocks of a major continent, can have that effect.

Punishing waves as high as buildings smash into the coast as I gaze upon nature's never-ending battle of unstoppable fluid meeting immovable solid. Feeling vulnerable and puny, I notice a warning sign, flattened on the ground up ahead. Walking along the coast, wisely sticking to the trails, I listen to the waves, feeling the atmosphere. There are no icebergs or whales this morning. No, on this day it's just the Atlantic — the mightiest of all oceans — and one humbled writer, greeting her waves before anyone else on an entire continent. An experience well worth getting up in the morning for.

START HERE: canadianbucketlist.com/capespear

THANK COD FOR BATTLE HARBOUR

Despite the name, there's no conflict placing Battle Harbour on our Atlantic Bucket List. I've never been anywhere quite like it. Sure, one can find restored historical villages and picturesque Atlantic fishing towns, but when the two blend together, surrounded by extraordinary subarctic beauty and infused with the comforts of a high-end hotel, the result is just the sort of destination you'll never forget.

Since history pounds the settlement into every flaking log, let's start with the past. Battle Harbour was founded as early as 1750 as a remote cod fishing community on Battle Island off the southeast coast of Labrador. For nearly two centuries, the community grew some, but not much changed. Abundant cod, seal, and salmon were harvested by schooners and brought into the protected harbour to be salted, packed, and shipped to Europe. The initial settlers were

British seamen, and over time some married local women and became *livyers* (for "live heres"). There were also *stationers* and *floaters*, seasonal schooners that would arrive each summer to trawl for the rich bounty of the North Atlantic. Labrador's first Marconi transmitter was set up, and at one point the island had the largest store in Labrador. In 1909, American explorer Robert Peary used Battle Harbour's transmitter to inform the world about his successful journey to the North Pole, and a small fishing village in Labrador became the focus of the world.

Located nine miles from the remote mainland, Battle Harbour might also have thrived because of the island's lack of biting insects. You don't have to spend too much time on the mainland to understand just what a blessing that is. By the 1970s, the isolated settlement was devastated by the collapse of the Atlantic cod industry.

Overfishing combined with new technology sank fisheries by the dozen, along with the coastal towns that supported them. Forced government relocation left ghost villages, as communities moved en masse to towns with services like schools and hospitals. Today, a smattering of locals return to refurbished old cottages in the summer, but most of the cabins and wharves are splintering with the memories of the past. Battle Harbour was no different until a non-profit Historic Trust decided to restore the community and transform it into a living museum. As the *Iceberg Hunter* ferry smashes into waves rolling into Mary's Harbour, I am eager to taste the fruits of their efforts. What will it feel like to stroll on the boardwalk of "them days"?

Grey skies, huge waves, and howling wind make for a memorable ferry crossing, but the protected cove of Battle Island ensures a smooth arrival. Restored clapboard houses face the inlet, a picture-perfect Atlantic Canada postcard. Overnight guests stay in two inns or a number of historical cottages. Included in the package is all meals, a guided tour, and ferry transport. Bags conveyed to the rooms, I enjoy the most delicious cod cakes I've ever tasted before Captain Jim Jones leads us new arrivals on a tour of the fisheries. Blackened fishing equipment is stacked in original storage sheds, the oldest dating back to 1771. We learn about the catching and curing of cod, the hard life of migrating seaman, shipwrecks, and sailing. Above us is the very room where Peary made his historic announcement. Life-size photos add to the ambiance. Some of you will love this history; perhaps others will prefer the exhilarating walk to the crest of the island, feeling the cold embrace of the Atlantic's wind, gazing at massive icebergs prowling on the horizon. Walking trails lead in every direction, and the island is too small to get lost. Soft, spongy terrain invites me to lie down among the blooming bakeapples, chomping on the berries, imagining patterns in the clouds above.

For a remote fishing settlement, the Harry Smith Room in the Mercantile Building is as comfortable as any high-end hotel, with soft robes, original paintings, and a lounge. There are, however, no phones, no TVs, and Wi-Fi is only available in the dining room.

There's also no need to lock the doors. Many guests will stay for one night, but I'm grateful I'll be here for two. The morning ferry departs back to the mainland shortly after breakfast, and I'm eager to hike the tundra landscape of Great Caribou Island, a short skip road across the tickle (a local term for channel). The sun's rays break through the clouds, brightening the plump orange bakeapples, shimmering off quartzite rock. The vista reminds me of Iceland, or scenes in *Game of Thrones* … the ones that look too beautiful to be real. After lunch, Captain Jim takes the Boston Whaler out to Cape Charles, where the bugs of the mainland attack.

"Back home, we call these birds," I tell him, having clapped out another mosquito.

Battle Harbour's bug-free zone is appreciated more than ever. The Whaler skirts around the island, and suddenly we are surrounded by a pod of orcas. Playful and curious, they gift me the best whale-watching experience I've had in Canada — not for lack of trying. Perhaps the secret lies in the lack of expectations. We didn't expect to see any whales, and that's why they showed up. Delighted by our luck, we take advantage of the last day of the recreational cod fishing season, and no sooner has my friend Jon lowered a jig than he pulls out a healthy-sized cod. Days like this you want to buy a lottery ticket.

After dinner, I'm standing by the old Marconi towers with Dave Landro, a guest from Edmonton. An egg-yolk sun is setting to our right; an unusually bright "super moon" is rising to our left. On the rocks below, Dave's pre-teen kids are playing with Noah, one of the local Labrador kids who summer on Battle Harbour. It's the sixth year the Landros have made the long journey from Alberta to spend their family holiday on Battle Harbour. They do it for the escape, for the freedom, for the beauty, and for the warm friendships they have struck with locals who breathe life into this historical community. Feeling the beauty and dread of the North Atlantic, watching those opposable orbs balance on celestial string, I make a silent vow to bring my family here one day too. It's been a magical forty-eight hours on a little island that truly belongs on everyone's Atlantic Canada Bucket List.

START HERE: canadianbucketlist.com/battleharbour

MAKE AN ICEBERG COCKTAIL

More than just the proverbial tip of an overused metaphor, let us salute the iceberg. Sinkers of unsinkable boats, stalking the oceans in search of prey for ironic disasters, icebergs are one of nature's finest works of art — transient, temporary, and just terrific in a vodka martini. There's a certain panache in mixing millennia-old pure crystal water melted from a roaming iceberg into any beverage. Take St. John's brewery Quidi Vidi's Iceberg beer. The label on its distinctive blue bottle reads: "Made with pure 25,000-year-old iceberg water." If you can apply freshness to beer, it certainly is one of the freshest beers I've ever tasted. The blue bottle further enhances the feeling you're actually drinking mineral water, until four bottles later you realize you're very drunk.

Thousands of years' worth of heavy, compressed snow break off from glaciers or ice shelves to form icebergs, and Newfoundland's Iceberg Alley is one of the best places in the world to see them — from land, boat, or kayak. Spring and early summer are the best viewing season, and so I find myself in the windswept seaside town of Twillingate, where iceberg tourism battles to save its ailing fishing industry. To fortify myself for the adventure ahead, I visit Auk Island Winery, which makes locally sourced wild berry wines. Four of their products are made with iceberg water, and the general manager, Danny Bath, assures me he can taste the difference. Inside their winery, a six-thousand-litre tank holds the iceberg water, and if you think that's a lot, you underestimate just how big these ice giants can be. A ship once recorded a 500,000-ton iceberg, while a small thirty-ton berg can provide a year's worth of fresh water for half a million people. You do, however, need a government licence to commercially harvest icebergs, more to protect consumers than for environmental reasons. Icebergs, therefore, don't need to be saved, just avoided should you happen to be captain of, say, a luxury cruise ship. Danny talks about the icebergs that arrive in Twillingate as if they were relatives visiting from Florida. "This one, he was a third of a mile long, I tell you, he was here for five weeks!"

Real Iceberg Vodka?

Canada produces a popular, world-class vodka made with the water of 10,000-year-old icebergs blended with Ontario sweet corn. Manufactured by the Newfoundland and Labrador Liquor Board, Iceberg vodka has won numerous international awards. The makers claim that iceberg water is seven thousand times purer than tap water, which eliminates the need for water purification. ➤

Thirst slaked, I feast on palm-sized fresh mussels at J&J Fishmarket (their fresh seafood platter deserves its own entry on the bucket list) and decide to enlist the help of local skipper Jim Gillard. Since the winds are strong and the rain hard, every operator in town has cancelled their iceberg tours. The friendly folks at the Anchor Inn suggest I call the Skipper, and he agrees to take me out on his seven-metre Seabreeze speedboat named *Galactic Mariner*. To find the Skipper, all I have to do is drive down Gillard Lane and look for a large observatory.

Skipper Jim was born and raised in Twillingate, a former meteorological technician for the navy and lifelong fisherman in these waters. He's also an astronomer with a mind-blowing homemade observatory complete with revolving dome (powered by Ski-Doo rails) and a thirty-centimetre LX200 Schmidt-Cassegrain telescope. Here's a guy with salt water in his blood and his head in the stars.

We don waterproofs and head out into the bay, rain stinging my eyes. Skipper Jim must have eye shields, for he's comfortably in his element. He talks about his navy days, fishing, the oceans, his kids, grandkids, whales, and icebergs. Skipper Jim's bucket list is telling: finish the shed, lay down the lobster traps, enjoy the stars. Here's a man who has everything he needs, right where he needs it. It takes about ten minutes before we see our target.

"Ninety percent of the iceberg sits under the water," says the Skipper, with that distinctive Newfoundland accent. Icebergs change every day, calving and cracking, with erosion forming distinctive

shapes as the ocean and shores gradually wear them down. Our "guest" today is about twenty metres high, with smooth lines, turquoise shades, and sharp peaks. It has also formed a flowerpot, much like the earthy examples on display at the Hopewell Rocks (see page 2). This dry-docked iceberg has the majestic design of a meta-snowflake, a true work of genius.

The Skipper keeps his distance. We can hear the ice cracking, which could cause a lower section to roll over and take our boat with it. He pulls up alongside a floating piece of ice and we haul a chunk on board. It is dense, white, and concrete heavy, unlike clear normal ice, thanks to the rain that has fallen into cracks. I take a knife and stab the top, the ice shattering into large pieces. The seas might be rough and the rain relentless, but I've come a long way to do this, and by golly you can't let a little weather stand in the way. Not in Canada.

I put the iceberg in a glass and pour some vodka on it. Calving a chunk of iceberg to make a cocktail is something to do before you die, I assure you. The vodka I used: Newfoundland's own Iceberg vodka, made, of course, with authentic iceberg water.

START HERE: canadianbucketlist.com/icebergcocktail

CATCH THE CONTINENTAL DRIFT

Arriving at the Gros Morne National Park Discovery Centre, I am ushered into a modern theatre to watch an introductory film about the region. There follow sweeping helicopter shots of epic landscapes straight out of *Lord of the Rings*, with attractive couples hiking on the edge of emerald-green cliffs. Cut to a scene that could have been shot in the fjords of Norway, with park interpreters and locals explaining in earnest voice-overs how this land has spirit, and once you experience it, that spirit will stay with you forever.

I'm always a little nervous about these introductory videos. They often set the bar too high, especially when I peer outside the window to see the now-familiar fog and rain. *Why is the weather always perfect in these videos?*

I walk around the centre, reading exhibits, learning about the geological wonderland of eastern Canada's second-largest park, a UNESCO World Heritage Site, where plate tectonics were first proven as fact. Atlantic Canada's second largest national park is 1,805 square kilometres in size, encompassing large mountains, forests,

shoreline, freshwater fjords, and bog, and yet it's hard to comprehend. Tell me that 500 million years ago the Earth's plates collided, forcing its mantle to split through its crust, resulting in Gros Morne's unique Tablelands, and all I see is a mountain of stone. Then I meet Cedric and Munju, two of the park's interpreters. We take a short drive to the Tablelands and stroll along its distinctly barren landscape. Cedric picks up a stone, and his French-Canadian accent drools with excitement.

"Each rock has a story, Robin, and the more we know, the more its story comes out." He begins to explain the basics of Gros Morne's importance in the world of science, its sheer uniqueness in our planet's time and space. Picking up a piece of rust-red serpentinite, he shows me how age-old minerals have been deposited on one side like the scales of a snake. Much like a battle plan, he uses rocks to demonstrate how the continents are continuously in flux. As he does so, the clouds begin to lift and the Tablelands loom above us in their glory, a moon mountain on Earth. There's not much time, so we jump in

the car and drive to Trout River, a cliché of a small Newfoundland fishing town.

"It's always worth driving through here," says Munju, "just to say hello to the characters." A man is barbecuing fat sausages inside his smoky garage, rain be damned. Gros Morne surrounds several fishing enclaves, where communities live as they have done for centuries. This is not Disneyland, and these are not re-enactors. The hard reality of the Atlantic fishing industry is on display, unusually located within a national park, and as fascinating to a "far away" like myself as the scenic beauty. Cedric takes us to a viewpoint over Trout River, the wind whipping up whitecaps across a freshwater lake. The ruggedness of the mountains and glacier-cut valleys is something to behold. We drop him off to return to his pregnant wife, and Munju invites me for some wine at her place, overlooking the inlet at Woody Point. She's just returned from Halifax after a seven-year hiatus and can't believe her magnificent view for the summer. Some friends arrive, and we head off to the Loft for tasty moose pie. It becomes clear that Gros Morne is more than just a park, it's a community; and yes, that community definitely has a spirit.

I bid my new friends adieu to make the drive to Rocky Point for the night. Since moose were introduced to the park, they have become quite a handful, especially for motorists. Earlier I had passed a sign on the Trans-Canada Highway that read, rather disturbingly: *660 Moose Collisions*. Around the park I'm advised to watch the ditches and pay attention, especially since I'm driving at dusk, when the moose are especially active. After my close encounter in St. John's

(see page 96), there's little doubt that moose through the windshield would not be as delicious as moose in a pastry.

After a week of rain, the sun at last breaks through for a glorious morning. Newfoundland has finally upgraded from a black-and-white TV to full-colour 3-D. It's a perfect day for the park's signature experience, a two-hour boat cruise up the Western Brook Pond. After I enjoy a relaxing half-hour walk over boardwalk and wild bog, the boat floats up this freshwater fjord between towering six-hundred-metre peaks and cascading waterfalls. The natural beauty rightly stuns everyone on board.

Yet it's not the Western Brook, nor the Tablelands, nor the great company in Woody Point I'll remember most. It's stopping off at Broom Point, walking ten minutes on Steve's Trail through a tree tunnel, and emerging at a panoramic view of the aquamarine coast, black mountains, and white beach all to myself. Damn it, that promotional film was right: there is a spirit to this place, and I'll never forget it.

START HERE: canadianbucketlist.com/grosmorne

Fjord: Go Further

During the last ice age, glaciers created the freshwater fjord of Western Brook Pond, a thirty-kilometre-long lake with one of the highest purity ratings for natural water. Boat rides are busy in the summer, so it's worth booking ahead. ➤

REWRITE THE HISTORY BOOKS

History is written by the victors, conquering their version of events into hard fact. Yet every once in a while the rug gets pulled out from under us, and we're forced to re-evaluate the past. For example: Every kid in America knows that Christopher Columbus was the first European to discover the New World, in 1492. Well, thanks to a couple of tenacious Norwegians and a little outpost on the northern tip of Newfoundland, the textbooks have been revised.

The Icelandic Sagas, dating back to the tenth and eleventh centuries, told stories of "Vinland," a land of wild grapes, located in the west beyond Iceland and Greenland. The sagas told how Vinland

was visited and settled by Vikings, although there was never any proof to back this up. Some theories suggest that, prior to Columbus, the Chinese traded with indigenous Americans, and even that Irish seamen traded on the American coast. A lack of physical evidence sinks as many theories as the Atlantic sinks boats. The fact that there exists a Central and South American demigod who sailed in from the ocean — tall, white, red-headed and -bearded — certainly suggests European influence in the Americas in ages past. Yet without proof, the historical record of Columbus held true.

In the 1960s, Norwegian adventurer Helge Ingstad and his archaeologist wife Anne Stine Ingstad combed the eastern coast of North America searching for physical evidence of Norse settlement. After many red herrings along a coast rich with cod, they happened upon a small, isolated fishing community called L'Anse aux Meadows. When they described to locals what they were looking for, they were surprised to be led to a series of raised mounds. The locals had attributed them to indigenous people, and the kids who played on them called them the Indian Camps. Over the next eight years, the Ingstads' excavations uncovered undeniable proof that this was, in fact, a Norse settlement dating back to CE 1000 — almost five hundred years before Columbus. Working in often brutal weather conditions, they discovered eight complete house sites and the

remains of a ninth. Parks Canada took over in the 1970s, and when UNESCO awarded its first World Heritage Site to Canada in 1978, the archaeological and historical significance of L'Anse aux Meadows won the day.

"Ya know, you definitely have some Viking in ya," says the colourful site interpreter, Clayton Colborne. (My blue eyes and red-tinged beard certainly suggest some interesting breeding in my European Jewish heritage.) Clayton was born and raised in the tiny community of L'Anse aux Meadows (population twenty-five) and used to play on the archaeological site as a kid. Today, his bearded, bright-eyed face adorns the Parks Canada pamphlet inside their modern Visitor Centre.

It's a grey, foggy day, but the drive here from Gros Morne National Park was pretty enough, dotted with fishing communities. The landscape looks like tundra, but Clayton tells me that's only because all the trees close to the road have been cut down. Homes still need a good supply of wood to make it through the long hard winter, and the nearest tree usually does the trick. Despite the solid tourism traffic, Clayton reckons the actual town of L'Anse aux Meadows — dating back to the mid-nineteenth century, when the French ruled the shoreline — will probably disappear. All the young folk have moved on.

After learning about Norse migration and other information from the Visitor Centre's exhibits, we walk along a wooden boardwalk into the field, passing beneath a striking sculpture called *The Meeting of Two Worlds*. "Full circle, ya know," explains Clayton. "When the Norse arrived and interacted with the locals, it was the first time two branches of humanity met in 100,000 years!"

Was L'Anse aux Meadows Vinland?

The latest archaeological evidence suggests that Vikings travelled south from L'Anse aux Meadows to the St. Lawrence River and into New Brunswick. Vinland, according to the Norse saga, was a country where wild grapes flourished, and New Brunswick is the northern limit for such grape varieties. Nobody knows why the Norse returned to their shipping base at L'Anse aux Meadows, packed up and sailed away to Greenland, never to return. ➤

All that remains of the excavations themselves are mounds, grassed over like burial plots. The Ingstads discovered many artifacts confirming Norse settlement, including a bone knitting needle, a bronze fastening pin, and nails made of a type of iron common in the British Isles. Farther along, Parks Canada has reconstructed a Norse hall, hut, and house out of sod, as they would have looked one thousand years ago. A re-enactor shares tales around a fire inside, and it isn't hard to imagine the cold, brutal conditions these early settlers had to endure. Perhaps this explains why the settlement was abandoned after a decade's use, the houses burned down. The Norse left, never to return. Perhaps this was only a way station en route to a larger, yet-to-be-discovered community, the Vinland so named because of the wild grapes that grew there. Perhaps it was abandoned because of a hostile relationship with the Natives, since we can agree Vikings were not the most peace-loving of people.

It's a mystery that remains to be solved. In any event, the only known evidence of European settlement in North America aged into obscurity until a Spaniard arrived hundreds of years later and reintroduced Europe to the "New World." In addition to experiencing the beauty of a stark landscape, and my new understanding of life from another millennia, I depart L'Anse aux Meadows enriched with Clayton's stories, and the satisfying feeling that a tiny Canadian village has proudly rewritten North American history.

START HERE: canadianbucketlist.com/lanse

SLEEP IN A LIGHTHOUSE

Paddling along the shoreline, Ed English gives me a lesson about Atlantic storms. "I went over to the West Coast and watched a storm blow in from the Pacific. They told me it was pretty bad, an eight or nine. Well, we kayak in those kind of waves."

Clearly, Ed is not your average hotelier, and his four-star Quirpon Lighthouse Inn is not your average hotel. Built in 1922 on the northernmost tip of Newfoundland, the lighthouse overlooks a natural passageway that creates a feeding ground for marine life. Migrating roughly three thousand kilometres south from Greenland, they're joined by floating hills of solid ice. This is the start of the province's Iceberg Alley, and one of the best places to see these natural marvels drifting on their slow, melting death march.

It's early June — peak iceberg season — as our kayaks skirt the seven-kilometre-long Quirpon Island. Ed bought the lighthouse in 1998, sight unseen, when it was put up for tender by the government. Despite wild weather and other challenges, he's turned it into a hotel that sleeps twenty-five guests in eleven rooms, from May to October.

Quirpon (pronounced *kar-poon*) has since received rave reviews, especially in international media. "Right now there's a couple from France, Japan, the U.S. . . . Sometimes I don't see Canadian guests until mid-July."

Seagulls are flying above us as the sun tiptoes into view from behind the clouds. We round another corner along the coast and there it is: a single dry-docked iceberg, boxed into the coast like a Viking helmet trapped at the end of a bowling alley. Its two icy peaks tower over us, the middle eroded to reflect water in a bright shade of blue. This mountain of compacted ice looks supernaturally out of place, ten thousand years of frozen water so pure that there's simply no trace of contaminants.

"Keep your distance, Robin. Towers like that crack off all the time, and besides the wave, you don't know how huge this is beneath us."

Icebergs come in all shapes and sizes — tabular, domed, pinnacled, wedged, dry-docked, and blocky — and watching them evolve from day to day is part of the fun. Yet Ed advises me never to turn my back on the ice, shape-shifting as it melts and smashes its way to oblivion on the rocks below. Kayakers should face forward, just in case.

We circle a couple of times, picking up some "bergie bits," small chunks floating in the water. My hands are numb from the cold, so we turn back to the harbour, taking advantage of the favourable wind and current.

Out of our wetsuits, we hop aboard the hotel's Zodiac to see if we can spot some whales. It's still early season, so it's unlikely, but it will give me a better look at the lighthouse from the sea, along with pairs of puffins clumsily flapping about us. It's calm as a lap pool when we leave, but within minutes we're cresting over three-metre swells. The water is choppy above the Labrador Current, the cold ocean current that flows south from the Arctic. With the icebergs come the whales — humpbacks, orcas, and other species. The bergs herd the fish into the island's coast, allowing guests to watch whales feed literally right below their feet.

Quirpon Island is rocky, mossy and barren, the lighthouse exposed like a palace guard defending the coast from attacking storms. When storms arrive, guests huddle up in excitement in the dining house, perhaps with hot chocolate and some bakeapple pie. Lighthouses are built to survive hurricane-force gales and monster waves, but the inn's location does present some challenges. Just last week, the wooden dock was smashed against the shore and is currently being repaired. As Ed points out the heliport, the Zodiac hits a swell and tilts upward at a 45-degree angle. We both pretend not to notice.

It's too early in the season and the wind is picking up, so he gratefully turns the Zodiac back to the small, protected harbour. Jacques Cartier and James Cook charted these very waters, and just up the road is L'Anse aux Meadows, where the continent's first visitors settled. With its history, wildlife, and adventure, Quirpon Island provides welcome shelter in the darkest of storms.

START HERE: canadianbucketlist.com/quirpon

GET SCREECHED IN

When Newfoundlanders heard I would be visiting the province for the first time, they didn't ask me if I would explore Gros Morne or track icebergs. They wanted to know if I would be getting screeched in. The fact that this tradition was born out of the St. John's bars on George Street, ready to charge you twelve bucks for the ceremony and certificate, is beside the point. To become an honorary Newfoundlander (not a Newfie, for that term is derogatory, unless you're a Newfie, in which case it's not), one must get screeched in.

Within a half-hour of my arrival in St. John's, I am at Trapper John's, a block from my hotel, just in time for the barkeep to begin

Deed I Is!

Since I assume you'll be "spirited" long before you decide it's a good idea to kiss a puffin's arse, practise the following line to endear yourself to your Newfoundland hosts.

When they ask you: "Is ye an honorary Newfoundlander?"
Reply, with gusto: "Deed I is me ol' cock, and long may your big jib draw!" ➤

the ceremony. Christian's, another bar in a city that likes its possessive apostrophes, apparently has a more authentic ritual, but they don't do it on Mondays, and this is Monday night. Thus I enter a mostly empty Trapper John's, where a couple from the U.K. and a student's mom are signed up for the evening's Screeching. To get screeched in, one must listen to the barkeep's bluster, drink a shot of screech, and then kiss a cod on the mouth — or, in the case of Trapper John's, the behind of a fluffy toy puffin. The screech in question is a type of cheap rum that hearkens back to days of yore when the same barrel might carry both rum and molasses. The sediment that remained would be fermented and mixed with grain alcohol to create a drink designed to blind a telescope. *Screech* was a term used for any moonshine, but it is now marketed as rum and consumed with great pride by locals — and by honorary locals, for that matter. It is so named because of the sound one makes after consuming it, or the sound in the flap of the sails on a boat, or whatever you're told by the local who will claim to know these things.

We line up at the bar and the bartender begins his story, which I struggle to understand. It is my first real exposure to the distinctive Newfoundland accent, which rolls like an English barrel, made of Canadian wood, down a Scottish hill. Something about the origins of the rum, aye aye this, ya ya that. We are then asked the following question: "Is ye an honorary Newfoundlander?" To which we must reply, with enthusiasm: "Deed I is me ol' cock, and long may your big jib draw!"

I shoot back the drink expecting a harsh burn down my throat, and am relieved to find it absent. Back in my university days, I indulged in Stroh rum, which at the time was 80 percent alcohol and could strip the innocence off a club of Girl Scouts. I've also had the misfortune to shoot straight absinthe in Denmark, raki in Albania, and 125-year-old moonshine in Georgia. Screech, by comparison, is palatable.

The toy puffin, representative of the province's official bird, has seen many lips, which the bartender goes to great pains to remind us. At this point I tell him about the far more intimidating Sour Toe Cocktail in Dawson City, which kinda punches a hole in his sails. He must hate travel writers. Still, I gamely kiss the butt of the fluffy puffin, receive a certificate, and that is that. A highlight of Newfoundland it was not, but at least I can tell Newfoundlanders that, yes, I have been screeched in. Despite the potential for hokiness, every province should have an honorary ritual for visitors. Undeniably, it makes you feel welcome.

START HERE: canadianbucketlist.com/screech

DRIVE THE TRANS-LABRADOR HIGHWAY

"Escaping it all" is an expression we can all relate to. It implies that we're locked away in a prison, behind restrictive high walls we have somehow constructed ourselves. Escape also denotes serious effort, one that is rewarded with invigorated freedom. Still, can this explain why anyone would drive 1,185 kilometres in almost complete isolation on potholed gravel roads renowned for shredding the very soul of an automobile?

The handy *Trans-Labrador Highway Guide*, provided by Labrador's Economic Development Board, has the answer on its front page: "For the adventure of driving through one of the last frontiers in North America. It is on our bucket list as the ultimate road trip." The TLH is the only road that crosses Canada's vast eastern mainland, as large as Japan, yet home to just 26,000 people. The highway has a notorious reputation, although steady roadwork in recent years has made it far more accessible, especially in the summer months. At least this is what I was telling myself, flying into Labrador City. My plan was to pick up an aptly named Ford Escape, hit the highway, and use the TLH as an excuse to tick off a Labradorean bucket list. I'd come armed with a bug vest, four cans

of bug dope, a travel companion with a penchant for meaningful conversation, and USB sticks loaded with music. With no cellphone service, we took advantage of the free loaner emergency satellite phones provided by the government, picked up and dropped off at participating hotels. When the friendly Filipino (there are a lot of Filipinos working in Lab City) at the Wabush Grenville Hotel front desk handed over the sat phone, we weren't sure if we should be comforted or spooked.

Lab City to Goose Bay, it turned out, is mostly paved, curvy blacktop, lacquered across the sprawling buggy boreal landscape. Our first roadside attraction is in Churchill Falls, the second largest underground power station in the world. Free tours depart daily into — location scouts take note — an excellent candidate for a James Bond villain lair. From this unusual company town, we drive east until we hit a sixty-kilometre gravel strip before arriving in the double-barrelled city of Happy Valley–Goose Bay. Between the mines and hydro projects, Labrador is enjoying an energy boom. "The province takes our money, but where is our road?" one local asks, referring to

The Viking Trail

Should the Trans-Labrador be too adventurous for your bucket list, substitute it with the Viking Trail. Running from Deer Lake to St. Anthony, this scenic 489-kilometre drive on smooth paved highway deserves its reputation as one of the world's most beautiful road trips. Tracing Newfoundland's west coast, the trail's highlights include Gros Morne National Park, the Arches, L'Anse Aux Meadows, and seasonal offshore icebergs. Explore the small towns, take long walks, and, if you're driving at dusk or dawn, look out for the moose. ➤

the dusty (or icy) reality of the region's transport artery. The state of the Trans-Labrador is a local obsession, although it seemed to please locals that we were crossing it with an urban SUV. Progress may be slow, but at least there is progress.

Labrador's cities have a distinct outpost feel to them. Be it Lab City's booming mines or Goose Bay's shrinking air force base, locals must bear harsh winters and hot, buggy summers. Visiting the cultural museum in North West River, or the aging Military Base Museum in Goose Bay, it's clear locals are desperately trying to preserve a fading historical legacy. Once we're back on the gravel road, I'm hoping the Escape's street tires will preserve their legacy, too, along with that of the windshield: transport trucks machine gun gravel when they roar past us, although fortuitously they are rare. Considering how much dust we leave in our wake, there are fortunately not too many cars either.

Sometimes, it feels like we're competing in the Paris-Dakar Rally. One-pump gas stations are few and far between, necessitating a fill-up at every opportunity. We veer off toward Cartwright, a small fishing community opened to the world with a new branch on the TLH in 2003. Pete and George Barrett's Experience Labrador Tours run boat trips to surrounding islands, and a sixty-five-kilometre-long beach known as the Wonderstrand. Against a backdrop of icebergs and velvet-green coloured hills, we pick sweet bakeapples in Little Packs Harbour, soaking in the Atlantic sun. Colours sharpen in this part of the world, as if your eyes have been tweaked like the viewfinder of binoculars. George reflects on "them days," regaling us with yarns. Understanding the distinctive Labradorean accent takes some practice, assuming you can decipher the local slang.

We backtrack a hundred kilometres to the junction and continue toward Port Hope Simpson, now comfortable enough at the wheel to barrel along the gravel. Officially the speed limit is seventy kilometres per hour, but drivers travel as fast as their nerves can handle. A sign indicates that we've now left Atlantic Time Zone and have gained the extra half-hour of Newfoundland Time. Several times we stop the car to admire the scenery, although leaving our mobile metal sanctuary brings an onslaught of blood-sucking black flies. Magnificent sunsets are best enjoyed at the wheel too. I've seen swallows smaller than Labrador mosquitoes.

The road deposits us in Mary's Harbour for our ferry to Battle Harbour (see Battle Harbour page 100), and continues along the coast toward Forteau. Approaching Red Bay, Canada's latest UNESCO World Heritage Site, gravel transforms to blacktop. Hundreds of kilometres of driving dust and noise, and suddenly we're floating on a road that feels as smooth as porcelain. With it, the wild remoteness of Labrador seems to dissipate. Road crews are busy re-paving all summer, and while sections of the road here are in the worst condition of the whole trip, it's smooth sailing all the way to Forteau. We climb the Port Amour Lighthouse (the tallest in Atlantic Canada), and try fly-fishing for the first time with Brad and his dad from Labrador Tours. It's important to make time for something new— even if the fish aren't biting.

Although the ferry to Newfoundland runs on Newfoundland Time, it departs from the Quebec town of Blanc-Sablon. Hey, if

trains in Russia can cross five time zones but run on Moscow Time, a rickety old ferry in Quebec can travel in time too. After some challenging fog and wind at the start of our journey, the St. Lawrence is as still as a glass of tap water. I settle down to write in the abandoned ferry bar upstairs, watching a baby humpback ripple the waters in the distance.

Barring incident, you can drive the entire length of the Trans-Labrador Highway in twenty-two hours, but that would diminish the best attraction of the road — the opportunity to escape to an oft-forgotten corner of Canada, where the characters, history, and landscape add up to a one-of-a-kind bucket list road trip adventure.

START HERE: canadianbucketlist.com/tlh

DISCOVER THE TWO B'S

Newfoundland and Labrador has no shortage of charming fishing towns, with wooden houses brightly painted against lush green cliffs, sweeping views of the Atlantic, and, if the commercials are anything to go by, unsupervised red-headed kids running about. While there are many wonderful places to visit, the bucket list focuses on the two Bs: Bonavista and Brigus.

Giovanni Caboto was an Italian explorer, sailing his fifty-ton, three-mast ship under a British flag. In 1497, he spotted North America after two months of sailing west on the Atlantic, famously declaring, "*O buena vista!*" Thus began the long history of an important fishing town, which once swelled to twenty thousand souls relying heavily on the Atlantic cod industry. Today, the town and rocky shoreline of Bonavista (population five thousand) is a historic landmark, site of John Cabot's first landing (Giovanni has been anglicized, much like my real name, Roberto Esrockavinni). Bonavista is known for its heritage buildings, museums, and famously welcoming locals.

What's with the Pink, White and Green?

You might notice a pink, white, and green flag flapping outside houses in St. John's. The Newfoundland tricolour is *not* the official flag of the province. It was created in the 1880s as the flag of a Roman Catholic group in St. John's, drawing on Irish influences, with the pink (or rose) strip possibly protesting against English Protestantism. The flag was controversially taken up by politicians and rabble-rousers, and gained in popularity in a British dominion that once debated whether or not to join Canada. More recently, there was a movement in St. John's to petition for the tricolour to gain official flag status, but a poll suggested the majority of Newfoundlanders were not tickled pink with the idea. ➤

Wander down Church Road, with its narrow sidestreets, watch for whales and icebergs from the lighthouse, explore the wharves and piers, learn about the salt fish trade, and hop aboard a full-scale replica of the *Matthew*, Cabot's ship that started it all.

Closer to St. John's is Brigus, a traditional English fishing village with a name derived from the word *brickhouse*. This should

give you some indication of the Scottish/Irish-influenced accent in this part of the world. Brigus dates back to 1612, when the town attracted English, Irish, and Welsh settlers. For a small town, it produced many famous Arctic sea captains in its day, such as Captain Bob Bartlett, whose former home is now the Hawthorne Cottage National Historic Site. Along with other Bartlett family heroes — John, Sam, Robert, Arthur, Isaac and William — Brigus captains were the first to reach the North Pole, sailing with Admiral Robert Peary, undertaking miracle rescues, and lighting the path for the shipping legacy of the Canadian Maritimes. Other Brigus attractions include the festive annual Blueberry Festival, Landfall's Kent College, year-round performances at St. George's Anglican Church, Ye Olde Stone Barn Museum, and the Tunnel, where early engineers used steel spikes and gunpowder to blast 24-metre-long holes in solid rock to provide easy access to Abram Bartlett's wharf. You may be in a rush to see Newfoundland, but Brigus wants you to stop, breathe, walk the narrow streets, admire the harbour, and chat with the locals.

Two Bs, representing two glimpses into the storied past of Newfoundland. Two places to take your time, feel the ocean breeze, and turn off the modern world.

START HERE: canadianbucketlist.com/bonavista

Not far from Brigus is Cupids, the oldest English colony in Canada, and the second English colony founded in North America. If you love the name, be further encouraged that it overlooks Conception Bay.

CHEW THE WHOLE SCALLOP

Ocean delicacies belong on our Atlantic Canada Bucket List. We tonged and shucked oysters, hauled and cracked lobsters. Next up is that muscularly white wonder of seafood candy we call the scallop. Breading and deep-frying does this living ocean fruit no justice. Nor does wrapping it in bacon and searing it with soy sauce — would you dare do such a thing to an oyster? As I was to discover at Aqua Labadie, an operational scallop farm located in Quebec but serviced by Labrador, scallops are best appreciated raw or poached in seawater, and always better shared in good company.

Agritours are fun, educational, and, in the case of scallops, rather delicious. Located in a largely unknown stretch of exquisite scenic beauty, heading west fifty kilometres from the Labrador border past the ferry town of Blanc Sablon, Aqua Labadie is the brainchild of Philippe and Clara Labadie. Through trial and error, Philippe learned how to successfully farm scallops, while Clara, inspired by a Champagne tour in France, is building their growing tourist operation. After all, it's not every day one sees how scallops are gathered, much less in a location as striking as Salmon Bay. Each

summer, when the tundra-lime hills roll into the sparkling Gulf of St. Lawrence, the Labadies invite tourists for a lifestyle tasting. It begins with a smooth boat ride up the channel on their luxury pontoon, passing abandoned fishing communities, a working fishery, and rocky beaches. During my visit, the sea is as smooth as porcelain, although admittedly this isn't always the case. Back on land, Philippe demonstrates how scallops can grow into the size of dinner plates, their age determined by lines on the shell — just like rings of a tree. I learn how they are carefully placed in nets to be protected from predators like starfish and lobster. When I pick up a live scallop, the shell opens and interacts. This is very much a living creature, with dozens of pinhead black eyeballs on its meaty exterior. Returning to the tastefully decorated tasting room, it's time to taste what all the fuss is about. Shell in hand, Philippe scrapes away the meat with a knife, leaving the familiar white muscle. He hands the shell over to me. Completely raw, as fresh as any seafood could possibly be.

"Go ahead, taste that."

I pop it into my mouth and savour the familiar texture, only juicer, and sweeter than any scallop I've tried before. Philippe is clearly proud of my reaction, proud of introducing visitors to the wonders of unfrozen, uncooked scallop.

Next, Clara has prepared a tasting tray of scallops on the shell, poached for two minutes in seawater and accompanied by a bake-apple and red berry drizzle. They are firmer, but just as delicious, especially with the sweet/sour condiments. Finally, it's time to taste the full meal deal — the muscle, meat, tendons, and caviar. All together, it looks unappetizing, as gizzards and organs and intestines often do. I get past my sight aversion and fork a chunk into my mouth. It tastes not unlike a large mussel sandwiching scallop meat. Delicious, although for aesthetic reasons, I don't expect full scallop to appear on many menus anytime soon.

Tours to Aqua Labadie are arranged through a company called Tour Labrador, or if you're mobile, drive north on the Jacques Cartier Highway from Blanc Sablon until you see the yellow signs. Tours typically last one to three hours, depending on what you go for, concluding with a tasting, or even a full seafood meal. I make a solemn promise to never again desecrate this morsel with breading and a deep fryer. That would be like deep-frying an apple. Canada salutes the Atlantic scallop, another homegrown culinary treasure we can all appreciate.

START HERE: canadianbucketlist.com/scallops

EPILOGUE

My travels have allowed me to learn a thing or two: The importance of smiling and not panicking in tricky situations. Trusting my instincts, keeping an open mind, and remembering to check my expectations with my baggage come in handy, too. But perhaps the most important nugget of wisdom I can impart is that it's the people we meet who create the paradise we find. Itineraries are an outline, but characters and personalities colour in the various shades of any journey. My single biggest piece of advice when it comes to tackling any experience in this book is simple: share it with good people, and if you're on your own, be open and friendly to those around you.

It's also worth noting that travel is as personal as your choice of underwear. You might not meet the folks I met, have the same weather, or enjoy each experience as much as I did. Your experience of Atlantic Canada is as unique as you are — even if you're only reading the pages of this book.

The Great Atlantic Canada Bucket List is a great start, but I'm well aware there are woeful omissions, places and experiences known and less-known that I haven't got to just yet. Some of them will pop up on canadianbucketlist.com, where you can let me know what I'm missing. I expect my Canadian bucket lists will keep growing in the years ahead, because the more we dig, the more we'll find, and the more we find, the more we can celebrate, sharing the best of Canada with locals and visitors alike.

Torngat Mountains National Park, fishing on the Miramachi, one-of-a-kind restaurants and hotels — there's always more to discover. Every chapter in this book concludes with two important words: **START HERE**. I'll end my Atlantic Canada Bucket List with two more: **START NOW**.

RE
robin@robinesrock.com

ACKNOWLEDGEMENTS

This bucket list is the result of many miles and many hours of travel, with the professional and personal help of many people and organizations. My deep gratitude to all below, along with all the airlines, ferries, trains, buses, hotels, B&Bs, and organizations who helped along the way.

NEW BRUNSWICK: Tourism New Brunswick, Alison Aiton, Margaret MacKenzie, Joan Meade, Kurt Gumushel, Jocelyn Chen, the traffic officer who pulled us over and didn't ruin our day.

PRINCE EDWARD ISLAND: Tourism Prince Edward Island, George Larter, Joe Kalmek, Keri May, Nathalie Gaultier, Ryan and Stacey Evans, Pat Deighan, Brenda Gallant, Isabel McDouggal, Robert Ferguson, Eza Paventi, Pamela Beck.

NOVA SCOTIA: Nova Scotia Tourism Agency, Destination Cape Breton, Pam Wambeck, Randy Brooks, Gregory Gallagher, Angelo Spinazzola, Gregory Gallagher, Wolfgang Greiner, Ludovic Bischoff, Parks Canada, Monica MacNeil

NEWFOUNDLAND and LABRADOR: Newfoundland and Labrador Tourism, Destination Labrador, Gillian Marx, Keith Small, Randy Letto, Jon Rothbart, Laura Walbourne, Janice Goudie, Ford Canada, Sarah Sullivan, Monica MacNeil, Nunatsiavut Group of Companies, Tour Labrador, Peter Bull, the Anchor Inn, Munju Ravindra, and that moose for not killing me.

SPECIAL THANKS: David Rock, Karen McMullin, Margaret Bryant, Kirk Howard, Carrie Gleason, Allison Hirst, Synora van Drine,

Courtney Horner, Hilary McMahon, Cathy Hirst, Jon Rothbart, Elyse Mailhot, Ian Mackenzie, Sean Aiken, Gary Kalmek, Joe Kalmek, Heather Taylor, Guy Theriault, Jennifer Burnell, Lauren More, Joshua Norton, Ann Campbell, Linda Bates, Patrick Crean, Gloria Loree, Ernst Flach, The Canadian Tourism Commission, Go Media Marketplace, Josephine Wasch, Ken Hegan, Jarrod Levitan, Vancouver and Burnaby Public Libraries, Zebunnisa Mirza, Sherill Sirrs, Chris Lee, Marc Telio, Brandon Furyk, RtCamp, Mary Rostad, the Kalmek and Esrock families.

SPECIAL THANKS TO THE FOLLOWING, WITHOUT WHOM THERE WOULD BE NO COMPANION WEBSITE OR SPEAKING TOURS: Ford Canada, Parks Canada, VIA Rail, Travel Manitoba, Tourism Saskatchewan, Tourism New Brunswick, Tourism Quebec, Tourism Prince Edward Island, World Expeditions, and Keen Footwear.

And finally, to my parents, Joe and Cheryl Kalmek (without whom there would be no Robin Esrock), my ever-supportive wife, Ana Carolina, and my daughter Raquel Ayla. *Yay! Aipane! Uppee!*

PHOTO CREDITS

COVER IMAGES:
Jon Rothbart; Peter C.; Ed English; Robin Esrock; Robin Esrock; Thinkstock; Robin Esrock; Linkum Tours (back cover)

AUTHOR PHOTO:
David Rock

MAPS: Mary Rostad

iii Matt Boulton; Robin Esrock; Scott Munn/ Nova Scotia Tourism Agency; Thinkstock
v Robin Esrock/ Ana Esrock

WALK THE SEABED BENEATH HOPEWELL ROCKS
2 Peter C.
3 Robin Esrock
4 Courtesy Tourism New Brunswick

JET-BOAT THE REVERSING FALLS
6 Courtesy Tourism New Brunswick
7 Courtesy Tourism New Brunswick

ABSEIL CAPE ENRAGE
10–11 Matt Boulton
12 Robin Esrock
13 Michelle Bailey, https://flic.kr/p/Mx8go. Licence at http://creativecommons.org/licenses/by/2.0

ROLL UP MAGNETIC HILL
14 Magnetic_Hill_Moncton_Reverse By Jim101 (Own work) [CC-BY-SA-3.0 (http://creativecommons.org/licenses/by-sa/3.0) via Wikimedia Commons

BIKE IN A KILT
15 Courtesy Tourism New Brunswick
16 Robin Esrock
17 Courtesy Tourism New Brunswick

APPRECIATE THE GENIUS OF DALI
18 Wikimedia Commons
20 Courtesy Tourism New Brunswick

WALK OFF A CLIFF
22 Joe Kalmek
24 Courtesy Tourism New Brunswick

CROSS HARTLAND'S COVERED BRIDGE
25 Robin Esrock
26 Courtesy Tourism New Brunswick
27 Hartland NB by Nile_Z, https://flic.kr/p/adjU8a. Licence at http://creativecommons.org/licenses/by/2.0

HIKE THE FUNDY FOOTPATH
28 P1130153 by Zach Kruzins, http://flic.kr/p/a7TRiD. Licence at http://creativecommons.org/licenses/by/2.0
29 Fundy Footpath by Leonora Enking, http://flic.kr/p/6HrhxE. Licence at http://creativecommons.org/licenses/by/2.0

ZIPLINE OVER A WATERFALL
30 Robin Esrock
32 Robin Esrock

PAINT YOUR FACE AT TINTAMARRE
33 Courtesy Tourism New Brunswick
35 Courtesy Tourism New Brunswick

DRINK A POTATO SMOOTHIE
37 Asma Regragui
39 Courtesy Potato World

RAFT A TIDAL WAVE
42 Courtesy Tidal Bore Rafting Park
44 Courtesy Tidal Bore Rafting Park

STROLL AROUND LUNENBURG
46 Courtesy Tourism Nova Scotia Agency
48 Thinkstock
48 Courtesy Tourism Nova Scotia Agency
49 Robin Esrock

ARM A CANNON AT THE HALIFAX CITADEL
50 Robin Esrock
51 Robin Esrock
52 Courtesy Tourism Nova Scotia Agency
53 Wikimedia Commons
53 Thomas Duff, https://flic.kr/p/asGSF6. Licence at http://creativecommons.org/licenses/by/2.0

ENJOY A SOCIABLE BEER
54 Robin Esrock
55 Thinkstock
56 Nicole Bratt, https://flic.kr/p/co6kmo. Licence at http://creativecommons.org/licenses/by/2.0
56 Robin Esrock

Run a Race of Biblical Proportions
57 Courtesy Tourism Nova Scotia Agency
59 Robin Esrock

Explore Cape Breton and the Cabot Trail
60 Courtesy Tourism Nova Scotia Agency
63 Robin Esrock

Have a Blast in Louisbourg
64 Robin Esrock
65 Robin Esrock

Cycle Across the Gentle Island
68 Robin Esrock
71 Robin Esrock

Haul a Lobster Trap
72 Robin Esrock
74 Robin Esrock

Tong and Shuck Oysters
76 Robin Esrock
78 Robin Esrock
79 Robin Esrock

Play a Round of Golf
80 Courtesy Tourism PEI
81 Robin Esrock
82 Thinkstock
83 Courtesy Tourism PEI

Cross Confederation Bridge
84 Robin Esrock
85 George Larter

Harvest Sea Plants
87 Thinkstock
89 Robin Esrock

Meet Anne of Green Gables
90 Courtesy Tourism PEI
91 Robin Esrock
92 Robin Esrock
93 Robin Esrock

Watch the Sun Rise on a Continent
96 Eric Harrison, https://flic.kr/p/8xshgu. Licence at http://creativecommons.org/licenses/by/2.0
97 Robin Esrock
98 Thinkstock
99 Kenny Louie, https://flic.kr/p/d9cXpY. Licence at http://creativecommons.org/licenses/by/2.0
99 Robin Esrock

Thank Cod for Battle Harbour
100 Robin Esrock
101 Robin Esrock
103 Robin Esrock

Make an Iceberg Cocktail
105 Courtesy of Linkum Tours
106 Robin Esrock
108 Courtesy Newfoundland and Labrador Tourism

Catch the Continental Drift
109 Courtesy Newfoundland and Labrador Tourism
110 Robin Esrock
111 Robin Esrock
112 Robin Esrock

Rewrite the History Books
114 Robin Esrock
115 Robin Esrock
116 Robin Esrock

Sleep in a Lighthouse
118 Linkum Tours
119 Linkum Tours
120 Linkum Tours

Get Screeched In
122 Dave Rock
123 Dave Rock

Drive the Trans-Labrador Highway
125 Robin Esrock
126 Robin Esrock
127 Robin Esrock
129 Robin Esrock

Discover the Two B's
130 Courtesy Newfoundland and Labrador Tourism
131 Thinkstock
132 Courtesy Newfoundland and Labrador Tourism/Barrett & McKay

Chew the Whole Scallop
133 Robin Esrock
134 Robin Esrock
135 Robin Esrock

MORE GREAT BUCKET LIST BOOKS BY ROBIN ESROCK

The Great Western Canada Bucket List

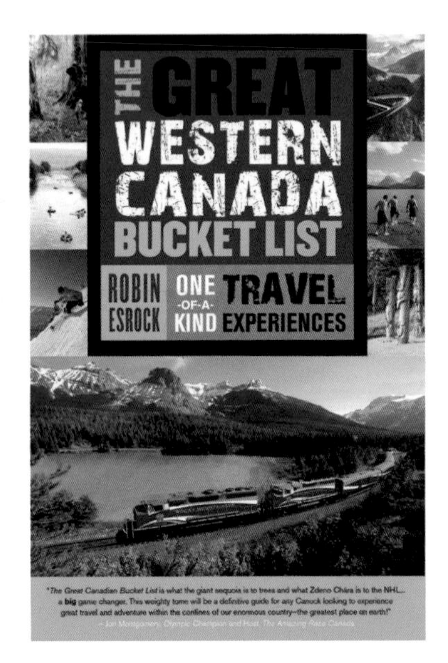

Most Canadians think of travel as a way to escape the snow, cold, and dreary winter skies. But Robin Esrock loves all that our western provinces have to offer, and so will you! *The Great Western Canada Bucket List* highlights some of the best travel experiences to be had on Canada's West Coast.

Through nature, food, culture, and history, as well as a few adrenaline rushes and some quirky Canadiana, Robin's personal quest to tick off the very best of Alberta and British Columbia packs in enough adventure for a lifetime.

Categorized by province, *The Great Western Canada Bucket List* will give you a first-hand perspective on:

- Sailing in Haida Gwaii.
- Tracking the spirit bear in B.C.'s Great Bear Rainforest.
- Wine-tasting in the Okanagan.
- Hunting for dinosaurs in Alberta's Badlands.
- Diving a sunken battleship.
- Snorkeling with salmon.
- Surviving the Calgary Stampede.
- RVing the Icefields Parkway.

The Great Central Canada Bucket List

Most Canadians think of travel as a way to escape the snow, cold, and dreary winter skies. But Robin Esrock loves all that the provinces of Ontario and Quebec have to offer, and so will you! *The Great Central Canada Bucket List* highlights the best travel experiences to be had in the heart of Canada.

Renowned travel writer and TV host Robin Esrock explored every inch of central Canada to craft the definitive Bucket List for the region. Running the gamut of nature, food, culture, history, adrenaline rushes, and quirky Canadiana, Robin's personal quest to tick off the very best of Ontario and Quebec packs in enough for a lifetime.

Categorized by province, *The Great Central Canada Bucket List* will give you a first-hand perspective on:

- Riding a motorcycle around Lake Superior.
- Drinking caribou with Bonhomme.
- Unravelling a mystery in Algonquin Park.
- Spending the night at an ice hotel.
- Scaling the via ferrata at Mont-Tremblant.
- Exploring the great museums.
- Cave-swimming in the Magdalen Islands.

DUNDURN